Adopted Children
Speaking

 **the information store**  📞**01603 773114**
email: tis@ccn.ac.uk

```
┌─────────────────────────────────────────┐
│ ║                                       ║ │
│ ║        21 DAY LOAN ITEM               ║ │
│ ║                                       ║ │
└─────────────────────────────────────────┘
```

Please return <u>on or before</u> the last date stamped above  **CITY COLLEGE NORWICH**

A fine will be charged for overdue items

D0540839

Notes about the authors

Caroline Thomas is a Research Fellow at Cardiff University. She took the lead role in this study of older children's views and experiences of the adoption process. She is currently on secondment to the Scottish Office managing a programme of research on the Children (Scotland) Act 1995.

Verna Beckford is a social worker with Bath and North East Somerset Council. She has worked as a Research Associate at the Bristol University's Norah Fry Research Centre and at Cardiff Law School. She is also co-author of *Consolidation or change? A second survey of family based respite care services in the United Kingdom* with C Robinson.

Nigel Lowe is a Professor of Law at Cardiff Law School. A former Chair of BAAF's Legal Group (1984–1990), he has a long-standing interest in adoption and, together with Professor Murch, has directed a number of empirical studies into its law and practice including *Supporting Adoption: Reframing the approach*. He has published extensively and is the co-author of *The Children Act in Practice* (2nd edn) with Richard White and Paul Carr, and of *Bromley's Family Law* (9th edn) with Gillian Douglas. He is an editor of *Clarke Hall and Morrison On Children* and of *Family Law Reports*.

Mervyn Murch has taught Law and Applied Social Studies and is a Professor of Law at Cardiff Law School. His 30 year research career has focused on the interdisciplinary work of the family justice system and has contributed to policy and practice development and law reform in divorce, adoption and child protection. He is currently studying the ways by which the voice of the child can be heard in divorce proceedings. His books include *Justice and Welfare in Divorce*, *The Family Justice System* with Douglas Hooper and *Grounds for Divorce* with G Davis.

Adopted Children Speaking

Caroline Thomas and
Verna Beckford
with
Nigel Lowe and
Mervyn Murch

British
Agencies
for **A**doption
and **F**ostering

Published by
British Agencies for Adoption & Fostering
(BAAF)
Skyline House
200 Union Street
London SE1 0LX

Charity Registration 275689

© Caroline Thomas, Verna Beckford,
Nigel Lowe, Mervyn Murch, 1999

British Library Cataloguing in Publication Data
A catalogue record for this book is available
from the British Library

ISBN 1 873868 78 2

BAAF is grateful to the Stanley Smith General
Charitable Trust for the generous donation
towards this publication.

Appendices designed by Martin Howard
Prompt cards © Martin Howard
Book and book cover designed by Andrew
Haig & Associates
Typeset by SMD
Printed by Russell Press Ltd (TU), Nottingham

Contents

Chapter 4: Matching and Introductions

Chapter 5: Moving

Chapter 6: Court

Chapter 7: Life Story Work

Chapter 8: Contact

Chapter 9: Adoptive Home and School

Chapter 10: Conclusion

References

Useful Organisations

Useful Books

Appendices

Preface

In the United Kingdom, as in the Western World as a whole, there is an increasing consciousness of children's rights. We now take a less paternalistic view of children. Today educationists, social scientists and policy makers are beginning to talk of children as "social actors", well able to shape and manage their own social worlds and cultures. In family law the Inquiry into the death of Maria Colwell (1974) and a whole subsequent tragic sequence of child abuse inquiries exposed the dangers of ignoring the voice of the child. The legislative remedy now finds expression in the requirement for courts to ascertain "the wishes and feelings of children" according to their age and level of understanding in all proceedings for adoption,[1] child protection,[2] and divorce involving children.[3] Moreover, Article 12 of the United Nations Convention on the Rights of the Child 1989, which has been ratified by the UK, requires that:

> States Parties shall assure to the child who is capable of forming his or her own views the right to express those views freely in all matters affecting the child, the views of the child being given due weight in accordance with the age and maturity of the
> child . . . The child shall in particular be provided the opportunity to be heard in any judicial and administrative proceedings affecting the child, either directly, or through a representative or appropriate body, in a manner consistent with the procedural rules of national law.

While the principle is accepted that children's voices should be listened to when legal and administrative authorities are taking decisions about them, and while it is true that specialist services such as the guardian *ad litem* service exist to give it effect, many questions remain about how best to translate principles into practice and procedure. Much depends on the adults' skills in communicating directly with children who, after all, inhabit quite different cultural worlds. Children can be baffled by the language of adults, especially by professional jargon. Equally, adults are often unfamiliar with children's language codes which, in any event, can differ

---

1   Adoption Act 1976, s 6.
2   Children Act 1989, s 1(3)(a).
3   Family Law Act 1996, s 11(4)(a), although whether this will be implemented is open to question.

i

from age group to age group. In the family justice system, for example, there are emerging practice debates on how to develop the communication skills required by children's representatives and about whether, and if so how, judges should see and listen to children when taking decisions about them. The prevailing practice in England and Wales is that they should not, in part because with the adversarial culture it is not possible to promise children that what they say to the judge will be treated in confidence.[4]

In social work too there is much concern about how best to develop skills in communicating with children. A recent study of social work training reported that:

> ... in spite of the fact that the majority of children entering local authority care or who are placed on supervision are now adolescents and young people, there were almost no references to courses targeting the skills and knowledge required to work with this age group and their families. (Marsh and Triseliotis, 1996, p. 183)

There is clearly, therefore, much that has to be done if we are to get beyond the rhetoric of legislative aspiration, and if we are genuinely to enable children to have a greater say in the processes which shape their futures. In this quest social research can play a vital developmental role as, we believe, this report shows.

Thus at Cardiff University the Family Law Research Unit of the Law School, in collaboration with colleagues from the University's recently established Inter-disciplinary Family Studies Research Centre, is developing a programme of projects focusing on the child's perspective of various legal and social work processes.[5] The primary authors of this particular adoption study, Caroline Thomas and Verna Beckford, have played a major pioneering role in this programme, developing, with the help of children themselves, various child-sensitive approaches which we, as the Directors of the project, believe have wider application in family law and social work.

Mervyn Murch   **Nigel Lowe**
Professor of Law   Professor of Law
Cardiff Law School   Cardiff Law School
Cardiff University   Cardiff University

The Autumn Equinox, 1999

---

4   Different judicial practices apply in European countries which operate more inquisitorial procedures, for example, France and Germany.
5   Other work includes an ESRC project, *Children's Perspectives and Experience of the Divorce Process*.

Acknowledgements

Our first debt is to the children and young people who enthusiastically helped with this research project. If they had not generously shared with us their personal experiences of the adoption process, this book could not have been written. We are also grateful to their parents for supporting their participation.

The research was undertaken principally for the benefit of the Department of Health (DoH) and for those officials engaged with the review of adoption law and the development of adoption policy and practice. It was funded by the Department and supported by a specifically constituted Advisory Committee chaired by Dr Carolyn Davis of the Department's Research and Development Division. Other members were Mike Brennan and Julia Ridgway of the DoH; Joan Fratter, Senior Practitioner at Barnardo's; Pennie Pennie, Assistant Director, Children and Families, London Borough of Lambeth; Jim Richards, Director, The Catholic Children's Society (Westminster); Alan Rushton, Senior Lecturer in Social Work, Institute of Psychiatry, Maudsley Hospital; Phillida Sawbridge OBE; Professor June Thoburn, School of Social Work, University of East Anglia. They have been an invaluable source of advice and positive criticism. Our warmest thanks to them all.

When the research was in its initial planning stage we consulted with academics with experience of research with children. The research benefited greatly from the advice we received from Dr Ann Phoenix, Lecturer in Psychology, Birkbeck College, University of London; Dr Carol Robinson, Senior Research Fellow at Norah Fry Research Unit, University of Bristol; Dr Hedy Cleaver, Senior Research Fellow at University of Leicester; Ian Butler, Senior Lecturer in Social Work, School of Social Sciences, Cardiff University; Liz Norford, Research Associate at University of East Anglia; Dr Marjorie Smith, Deputy Director of Thomas Coram Research Centre, Institute of Education, London University; Marion Brandon, Lecturer in Social Work, University of East Anglia; Sue Rolfe, Research Associate, Centre for Family Policy and Child Welfare, School for Policy Studies, University of Bristol; and Dr Ruth Townsley, Research Fellow, Norah Fry Research Centre, University of Bristol.

During the planning stages of our study, we also consulted children of a similar age to those in our sample, and their parents. We thank Ellie (8) and Bron (12) and their mum, Lou; Solonge (10) and Monique (14), and their mum Grassarah; William (8) and Michael (13) and their mum, Becky; Laurie (15) and his dad, Brian; Lucy (12) and her mum, Jenny; and Zoe, Rachel, Annabel and Sophie (each 12 or 13). Our thanks also extend to Bristol members of Parent to Parent Information on Adoption

Services (PPIAS) (now called Adoption UK) who valuably commented on our research tools.

We are very grateful to Martin Howard for his graphic design and communication advice; Bridget Summers who arranged the project logo competition, and the children of Colston's Primary School, Bristol, who participated; and our sound recorder, Will Slater.

We benefited from discussing our methodology with friends and colleagues currently working in the fields of fostering and adoption, and special needs teaching, and would particularly like to thank Brian Robathan, Pam Fudge, Rose Mulligan, Sonia Dixon-Carter and Jane Parrish for informally sharing their expertise.

We also received valuable help and support from other members of the Support Services for Families of Older Children Adopted Out of Care project research team – Margaret Borkowski, Anna Weaver and Elizabeth Caddy. We must particularly thank Elizabeth, along with Jenny Saddington and Wendy Dear, for their painstaking transcriptions of the interviews.

Caroline Thomas
Verna Beckford
Mervyn Murch
Nigel Lowe

1 Background to the Research

INTRODUCTION

Adopted Children Speaking is a study of children's and young people's views and experiences of the adoption process and the support they received during that process. It focuses on the experiences of older adopted children who have previously been looked after by local authorities. As far as we are aware, it is the first study to focus on the adoption process and support issues from the children's point of view.[1]

This study is part of a wider research project published under the title *Supporting Adoption: Reframing the approach* (hereinafter referred to as the *Supporting Adoption* study or referenced as Lowe and Murch, 1999), funded by the Department of Health (DoH) and conducted at Cardiff Law School, Cardiff University, between January 1994 and May 1998. This research was intended to throw light on aspects of policy and practice concerning the support available to older children and their families as the children make the transition from being looked after by the local authority into a new life with adoptive parents. It does so from the perspectives of adoption agencies and adoptive parents. *Adopted Children Speaking* adds the perspective of the children themselves.

We set out to understand the children's experiences "in their own terms", and to take their words at face value, as the primary source of knowledge about their experiences (Marrow and Richards, 1996). In doing so we have effectively gone against a tradition in social science in which children's voices are rarely heard. Our approach, however, can be linked to a strand of social research, associated with Butler and Williamson (1994), concerned with 'hearing the voices of children, untrammelled by professional direction or interpretation'.

In reporting our data we have taken a descriptively-orientated approach (Wolcott, 1990, pp 27–30), and have not interrupted the children's

---

1   Other studies of permanent child placement have included some interview data from children about the adoption process; see Thoburn (1990) and Thoburn, Murdoch and O'Brien (1986).

account of their experiences with much adult comment and interpretation. To avoid distracting the reader from what the children had to say, the comment in the findings chapters has been kept to a minimum. In the last chapter of the report, however, we shift to consider the implications of the findings for policy and practice.

UNDERSTANDING OLDER ADOPTED CHILDREN'S NEEDS FOR SUPPORT

Children adopted after being "looked after"[2] by the local authority are likely to have had difficult pasts. Some may have suffered neglect or ill treatment before leaving the care of their birth families. Others may have experienced physical, sexual or emotional abuse. However they came to be looked after by a local authority, just over half will have spent five or more years in a variety of foster and community homes prior to their adoptive placements. Many will have experienced several moves, changes of school, and losses of friends. Adoption means another major upheaval affecting almost every aspect of their lives. It involves them in a process which is known to be protracted and fraught with uncertainties.[3] It is therefore vitally important that children who have already experienced such difficulties receive sensitive and appropriate support to help them through the adoption process.

THE AIMS OF THE STUDY

The overall aim of the study was to contribute to the development of knowledge and understanding of children's views and experiences of the adoption process and their support needs.

We felt it appropriate to take a qualitative approach given that the children's perspectives of the process and support issues have not been studied before. Such an approach also allowed the children to direct the study into areas they saw as significant. This possibility was important because children's perceptions as users and recipients of services are influenced by different considerations from those of professionals who provide them (Cloke and Davis, 1995).

---

2 I.e. children previously accommodated by a local authority and those in formal care under a care order.

3 See Lowe and Murch (1999), Part II.

The purpose of the study was to inform the Department of Health's review of adoption law, policy and practice. In addition, we intended the research to inform the wider community of policy makers and practitioners, particularly social workers and other professionals working in the educational and family justice systems, who are involved in the lives of adopted children. We hope that the findings will be of interest to foster carers, adoptive parents, and adopted children themselves.

The study also aimed to make a contribution to the expanding knowledge of children's lives, both within families and in other social contexts, arising from a growing number of UK studies across the social sciences which focus on children as social actors. These studies examine children as active agents, influencing as well as being influenced by the world they live in.[4]

The study should also be seen in the context of a key policy development in the last decade to consult children and young people and involve them in the planning and development of services that directly affect them. This has been officially encouraged in several ways (Ward, 1997). The Adoption Act 1976 refers to the need to give due consideration to children's wishes and feelings about adoption.[5] The House of Lords ruling in the *Gillick* case seemed to indicate that children who are competent to make a decision affecting their lives are entitled to do so.[6] In December 1991, the UK government ratified the United Nations Convention on the Rights of the Child; Article 12 recognises in principle the right of capable children to express views freely in all matters affecting them. The Children Act 1989 also embodies a number of key principles that demonstrate respect for the views of children. The Act requires that courts consider the wishes and feelings of children when making decisions concerning their welfare.[7] The desirability of involving children in matters that have an impact on them has also been recognised within the National Health Service and Community Care Act 1990.

---

4   For instance, in 1996, the ESRC funded 22 such projects within a programme entitled "The Children 5-16 Research Programme: Growing into the Twenty First Century". One of these, *Children's Perspectives and Experience of the Divorce Process*, is taking place within Cardiff University's Family Studies Research Centre.

5   Adoption Act 1976, s 6.

6   *Gillick v West Norfolk and Wisbech Area Health Authority* [1986] AC 112. But note the subsequent restrictive interpretation by the Court of Appeal in *Re W (A Minor) (Medical Treatment: Court's Jurisdiction)* [1993] Fam 64.

7   Children Act 1989, s 1(3)(a).

KEY RESEARCH QUESTIONS

Although the research was essentially exploratory, it was framed around the following key research questions:

- How do older children understand the process of adoption?
- What support do the children receive from peers, family and formal support services before, during and after their placement?
- What do they think of the help and support they received?
- Did they have any unmet support needs?
- Who do the children regard as the most suitable providers of support and comfort?
- Did the children feel they had opportunities to express their wishes and feelings about their whole adoption experience to professionals, and family and friends?
- If so, did they take those opportunities?
- If they expressed their wishes and feelings, did the children feel they were taken into account?

BOUNDARIES OF THE RESEARCH

Initially, we intended to focus on the children's views of the support they received from the time adoption was first suggested to them, through the transition out of local authority care or accommodation into life within an adoptive home, to the making of an adoption order. More particularly, for the purposes of this study, we broke the process down into four stages: being introduced to the idea of adoption and pre-placement preparation; matching and introductions; moving; and going to court.[8] However, retaining our focus on support issues, we subsequently extended our inquiry to include their views of their contact arrangements; life story work; and the support they were currently receiving at home and school. Nevertheless, it is important to stress at the outset that this book is not about children's views of *post adoption support* per se.

This study is concerned with the views of *older* adopted children, i.e.

---

8   In defining the process in this way, however, we acknowledge that there are many events and decisions taken earlier in the children's lives that are relevant to them being adopted. We also appreciate that after a court makes an adoption order, the process of adoption will continue for all parties for the rest of their lives.

those who were adopted at the age of five or over (to distinguish them from babies and infants), who had previously been looked after by the local authority. We were interested in formal services provided by adoption agencies (both statutory and voluntary) and by social, educational, health and psychological services. We also wanted to explore informal support such as that provided by families, friends, relatives and self-help groups, and previous carers of the adopted children.

We concentrated on children whose placements were ongoing. Resource constraints prevented the tracing and contacting of children who had experienced disruptions.[9]

THE INTERVIEW DATA

Throughout, the research was designed to be sensitive to the needs and wishes of the children. For the interviews we developed a framework for inquiry and discussion. Being aware that children had different placement histories, we anticipated that not all questions within the framework would be relevant to all children. For instance, we knew from parental interviews that some children initially knew their adoptive parents as foster carers. Therefore, once we had clarified that these children were not aware of other families having been considered for them, it was then inappropriate to ask them questions about waiting for an adoptive family.

Some children did not remember all parts of the process: they may have simply forgotten about them because they were very young or the relevant events occurred a long time ago or both. Others may not have had clear memories because of painful experiences. Furthermore, parts of the process held a different significance for different children. We also usually could not ask the questions in the order that seemed logical to us – questions about planning and preparation for adoption followed by matching, then moving and finally going to court. As Butler and Williamson (1994, p.30) explained, 'Children jump around and researchers have to jump around with them, seizing opportunities to probe and explore issues further'.

---

9   The researchers are hoping to conduct a further study which will focus on the views and experiences of children and young people who have been through disruptions. Such a study would be valuable in its own right, but much could also be learnt from comparing some of its findings with the views and experiences of the 41 children whose placements are ongoing, reported here.

For example, some children were deeply affected by the experience of going to court. In their keenness to talk about it they introduced the topic early in the interview. As children "jumped around" it was sometimes difficult to weave in all the topics. Some children also tired easily or lost concentration. One of the youngest in the sample, for instance, enthusiastically began to participate in the Family and Friends exercise, but quickly became exhausted. He was interviewed with his older brother and allowed his brother to take over most of the rest of the interview. For a while the younger boy quietly lay down on the floor beside the interviewer to rest, occasionally interrupting his brother to make a small contribution.

Although most children were enthusiastic and co-operative about taking part in the study, there were three children we found particularly challenging to interview. Two of them expressed a mixture of irritation, anger and hostility towards their interviewer and another was easily distracted and seemed to have great difficulties concentrating.

Overall, it was rare for a child to cover all possible topics.

2   Methodology

INTRODUCTION

The following detailed description of the development and use of our research tools reflects the time and effort we invested in them. It also emphasises our view that the communication methods we used will be of interest to practitioners who work directly with children in child care and the family justice system.

DEVELOPMENT OF THE RESEARCH TOOLS

Consultation

The research tools included:

- an Introductory Pack for adoptive parents, including a letter and fact sheet;
- a Children's Invitation Pack, including a leaflet and complementary audiotape;
- a consent form;
- a questionnaire; and
- a set of prompt cards.

These were developed in consultation with other researchers[1] who had experience of interviewing children. We also discussed them with children, both white and black, aged between 8 and 14, individually and in small groups, and with their parents. The tools were also developed with the help of social work practitioners, a graphic designer, a teacher of children with special needs, and our own friends and families. We also studied a selection of children's and young people's books and magazines.

   The tools were then piloted with three adoptive families contacted through Parent to Parent Information on Adoption Services (PPIAS) (now Adoption UK), a self-help organisation for adoptive families. They were

---

1   See Acknowledgements for details of consultants.

edited in the light of the piloting exercise and feedback from the project Advisory Committee.

Project logo

During the consultation period we were shown a logo for another children's research project, designed by children, which had been very popular with those who had participated in the study. We therefore arranged for about 40 primary school children to design logos for *Adopted Children Speaking*. One stood out from all the others which appealed equally to:

- boys and girls;
- children of all ages; and
- children from different ethnic backgrounds.

Our choice was supported by the children we consulted who were attracted to the logo's colours, which they explained were the current fashion colours. The design, called "Smiles", was used for the project letterhead and all the research tools (see Appendices A–I, K) and is also used on the cover of this book.

Introductory pack for adoptive parents

An introductory pack was developed for the adoptive parents which contained two letters, a fact sheet about the project, and a response form. Examples can be found in Appendices A, B, C and D. One letter re-introduced the parents to the *Supporting Adoption* study (Lowe and Murch, 1999). The other sought their support for their children's participation.

The fact sheet outlined the project's aims and researchers' approach. It described the arrangements and format for interviews and also indicated which stages of the adoption process were of interest. The sheet also described the contents of the enclosed *Children's Invitation Pack* and offered reassurance about consent and confidentiality. The fact sheet provided essential background information to enable parents to come to an informed decision about their children's participation. Parents were invited to contact us if they had any questions about the research.

Parental response

About 50 per cent of the parents who received the invitation packs passed them on to their children. Even though some parents did not agree to the participation of their own children, they expressed their general support for the research and wished us luck. We were encouraged that most of the parents who decided not to give their children the packs explained their decisions:

- There had been a serious illness in the family.
- The family had just moved or were about to move and the children were feeling unsettled.
- The placement was not going well – things were difficult, at crisis point.
- The placement had disrupted.
- The children's special needs were, in the parents' view, too severe and the children would not understand.
- The family was too busy.
- The placements were going very well.

The distribution of their responses is shown in Figure 1 below. The most common reason parents gave was that the placement was in difficulty. Seven families indicated that placements had disrupted.

We were surprised by two parents' explanations that they did not want to give the information about the project to their children because the placements were going very well and explored this further. Both parents explained that, in their view, their adopted children were so well integrated in their families that they no longer regarded themselves as adopted. The parents therefore did not want to remind the children of their adopted status by raising with them the possibility of their participation in the research.

Figure 1

Reasons given by parents for not passing on invitations

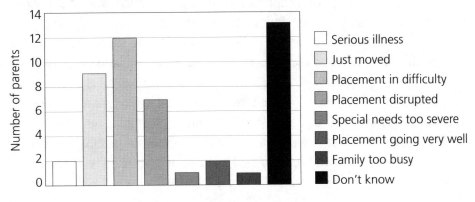

Children's Invitation Pack

These packs (see Appendices E, F and G) contained a leaflet and tape to let children know:

- who we were;
- where we worked;
- why we wanted to speak to them;
- what we wanted to talk to them about;
- answers to possible questions;
- that they could contact us if they wanted to ask us any other questions; and
- that if they were not sure whether to take part, they could talk to someone else to help them make up their minds.

To help the children make informed decisions about their participation it was vital to communicate information about the project appropriately. Children are increasingly used to sophisticated methods of communication so it was important that our resources should reflect this trend. With the help of a professional designer, we therefore adopted a modern approach. The appeal of the logo was used on the front cover of the leaflet to draw the children into the inside pages, like the cover of a book. The inner pages were kept simple so that the children were not distracted from the main message. We also used:

- short sentences;
- simple language;
- a clear educational typeface; and
- colour and graphics.

The leaflet included a photograph of the researchers which gave the children the opportunity to see them prior to the interviews. Although when we visited the children's homes we were essentially strangers, its inclusion meant that at least our faces were familiar. How we looked may have worked to our advantage or disadvantage according to the children's personal likes and dislikes. Age differences inevitably create barriers, but it was not possible to disguise our "thirty-something" years. The photograph on the back of the leaflet was chosen by three separate groups of children from a selection of about 50. They said it appealed because the interviewers looked especially happy, kind and friendly.

The tape offered *all* children a clear explanation of both the project aims and their potential contribution including:

- children who did not enjoy reading;
- children who could not read; and
- children with learning difficulties.

It also gave the children an opportunity to hear the researchers' voices in advance of interviews so that we were familiar to them in another way. However, how we sounded – tones of voice and accents – may have worked for or against us.

For introductory music, we considered using a few bars of music from the charts that the children would recognise and explored some of the copyright issues. By consulting children, however, we were reminded that their musical tastes are varied. So rather than risk using music that some children would have already decided they disliked, a sound recordist mixed a few bars of original music.

At the end of the interviews we asked the children what they thought of the tape and leaflet. The majority were very positive about them and said they were 'good'. Even children who enjoyed reading said they appreciated the tape. A 14-year-old boy was positive about both the tape and leaflet:

> *I read through the leaflet and listened to the tape and I*
> *understood all the questions and how we could change our minds*
> *if we wanted to. It made me understand what you were – what it*
> *was all about – and why you wanted to do us . . . and make it*
> *easy for other kids. I thought it would be quite a good idea . . .*

Several children mentioned that they listened to the tape several times. A girl (aged 10) said she thought it could have been improved by the use of more simple words and slower speech. The only other reservation about the tape was expressed by another girl (aged 12). The title of the project, *Adopted Children Speaking*, confused her and led her to expect to hear children's voices.

Costs

We were mindful of the costs involved in producing these materials. All the printed resources were designed in *Word for Windows* and produced in-house using the research unit's colour inkjet printer. The tape was also duplicated in-house.

Children's responses

Eighty-three per cent of the children who received invitations wanted to participate. (Unfortunately we do not know what the children who decided not to take part thought of the invitation pack.) Although we gave no indication that we wanted the tapes returned, the children were often keen to know if they could keep them.

THE SAMPLE

Selecting the sample

A total of 57 families were contacted about the possibility of interviewing their adopted children which resulted in a final interview sample of 41 children.

The original sample

The *Supporting Adoption* study (Lowe and Murch, 1999, p. 71) included 48 interviews with adoptive parents – couples or single adopters. At the end of these interviews, parents were asked if they were willing to be contacted at a later date about the possibility of interviewing their adopted children. The majority (40 out of 48) of them agreed. These 40 families had between them adopted 73 children.

We gathered information about the gender, age, ethnicity and special needs of these children from the questionnaires completed by their adoptive parents during the course of the *Supporting Adoption* study.

There were about equal numbers of boys and girls, mostly aged eight or over, clustered around the ages of nine to twelve. Six children were of mixed heritage. English was the first language in all 40 families. About one third of the children, according to their parents, had learning difficulties, three with moderate or severe learning difficulties. Approximately one third of the children had some behavioural difficulties. Parents noted additionally that one third of the children had special emotional needs. Some of the children had more than one kind of special need.

Twenty of these families participated, including 27 children. It was not, however, possible to meet our target of 40 interviews from this sample.

The additional sample

An additional 17 adoptive parents were therefore contacted from the 226 families in the *Supporting Adoption* study postal survey who had indicated a willingness to be interviewed, but who were not.[2] All the potential participants from minority ethnic backgrounds had already been included in the first sample. Therefore, all the adoptive parents in these 226 families were those who had classified themselves and their children as white. The 17 selected families had adopted 25 children, including 14 girls and 11 boys. About one quarter of the children had learning difficulties and a similar proportion had special behavioural needs. Just over one third of the children had special emotional needs. As with our original cohort, some of the parents classified the children as having more than one type of special need.

Eight families from this additional cohort, including 14 children, took part in the study.

Characteristics of the final sample

The final sample of 41 children included 25 girls and 16 boys. The bias in favour of girls was due to parents passing more invitations to participate in the project to girls rather than boys. Of the children themselves who considered taking part, proportionately as many boys as girls agreed to be interviewed.

Most children were white and placed with white families. Four children were of mixed heritage – one was in a same-race placement and the other three were placed transracially.

Some of the children had special needs. Their parents informed us that eight had special learning needs. The same number of children had behavioural difficulties and nine had emotional special needs. Two of the children had physical disabilities.

Characteristics of the children at placement

Questionnaires completed by adoptive parents for the *Supporting Adoption* study provided us with some further information about the sample.

Thirty-two of the 41 children were placed for adoption, but six were initially placed with long-term foster carers who subsequently decided to apply for adoption. There were also three children whose short-term foster placements evolved into long-term foster placements before becoming adoptive ones.

---

2   These additional families were selected on the basis of them living within 200 miles of our base in Cardiff, to keep within our budget for travel.

Twenty of the children were placed singly of whom ten had siblings placed in other adoptive and foster families. The other 21 children were placed in sibling groups – nine pairs and one group of three. Twelve children were adopted by families with other adopted children. Five joined families with other children who were being fostered. Six children became part of families which included children who were the adopters' birth children.

The mean age at placement for the whole sample was 5 years 10 months, ranging from 2 months to 10 years 4 months. The distribution of ages at placement for the whole sample is shown in Figure 2.

Figure 2
Age at placement – 41 cases

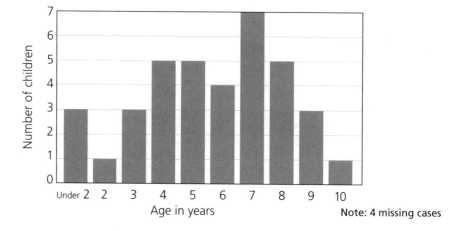

Note: 4 missing cases

As noted above, there were 32 cases where the purpose of placement was adoption. The average age at placement for this sub-sample was 6 years 8 months with a range from 2 years 11 months to 10 years 4 months. The distribution of ages at placement for this sub-sample is shown in Figure 3.

Once in placement, on average the children waited 2 years 4 months before their adoption orders were made. The minimum time period was 11 months and the maximum was 5 years 4 months (see Figure 4). The mean length of time was slightly lower, i.e. 2 years 1 month, for the 32 cases where the original purpose of the placement was adoption.

Figure 3
Age at placement – 32 cases

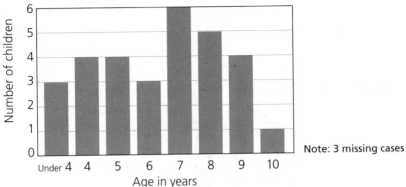

Note: 3 missing cases

Figure 4
Time period between placement and adoption order – 41 cases

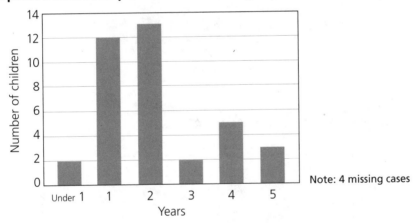

Note: 4 missing cases

Characteristics of the children at interview

At the time of the interview, the children were aged between 8 and 15, but most of them (83 per cent) were between 8 and 12. Figure 5 shows the distribution of the children's ages at interview.

When the children were interviewed, they had on average been in placement for 5 years 8 months. The time periods ranged from 2 years 4 months to 11 years 2 months.

The full distribution of the length of time the children had been in placement at the time of interview is shown in Figure 6. When the cases which began as foster placements are excluded, the mean period in placement falls to 4 years 10 months.

Figure 5
Age at interview – 41 cases

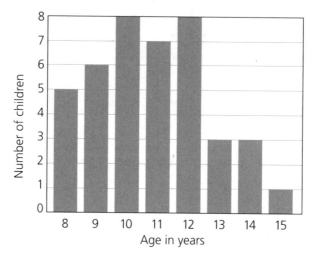

Figure 6
Time in placement at interview – 41 cases

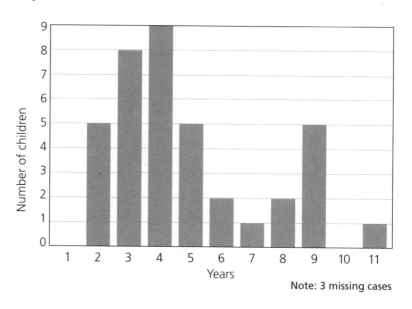

Note: 3 missing cases

All 41 children were interviewed after their adoption orders had been made. Figure 7 illustrates the time period between the making of the adoption order to the interview for the whole sample. The average length of time was 2 years 10 months. This average declines to 2 years 6 months for the 32 cases where the original purpose of the placement was adoption.

Figure 7
Time from the making of the adoption order to interview – 41 cases

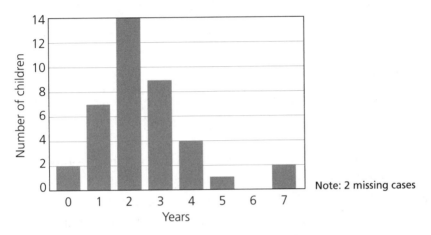

Note: 2 missing cases

INTERVIEWS

Introduction

The interviews were conducted between December 1996 and September 1997. Their duration varied, the average time was one-and-a-half hours. The shortest was 25 minutes and the longest took two hours. All the interviews were conducted in the children's homes. On arrival the interviewers spent a short time with the children together with their adoptive parents. Hopefully, this reassured the children that their parents supported their participation. However, we were aware that the more friendly with the adoptive parents we appeared, the more difficult it might have been for the children to be open with us about their adoptive placements.

The majority of the children were interviewed alone, in private. Three interviews involved talking to siblings in pairs because the younger siblings felt a little shy. Another three took place with their mothers present at the children's request. One mother, whose child had had an upsetting experience with his guardian *ad litem*, was present at the beginning of the interview, but left when she was reassured that the child was comfortable. Two interviews took place with parents within earshot, on occasions putting their heads round doors to ask the children if they wanted something to eat or drink. The interviews were a four-stage process consisting of:

- a warm up;
- family and friends;
- main questions and themes; and
- ending the interview.

Warm up

While we unpacked and prepared our resources, usually with the children's help, we chatted and answered any questions the children had about us or the interview itself.

We then explained again that we wanted to tape the interview so that we could remember exactly what they said. We also let them know that the tape would be kept safely. We added that a woman who worked with us would also listen to it and type a written record of the interview, and that this transcript would be kept safe as well.

The issue of the confidentiality of the tape was clearly important to some of the children. One girl (aged 11) raised it herself by asking,

Girl   *Will you let other children listen to that?*

Interviewer   *Listen to your tape? No. The only people who will hear it will be the people that I work with.*

Girl   *Ah ha. It's not that, I don't mind, but I just . . . [pause].*

Interviewer   *You'd like to know?*

Girl   *Yeah.*

Only two children did not wish to have their interviews tape-recorded. One of these children agreed to her interviewer taking a few notes during the interview. The other focused on the Family and Friends exercise and she allowed her interviewer to keep the eco map as a record of the interview. As soon as possible after these two interviews, the interviewers made fuller records from memory of what was said.

If the children agreed to be recorded, we then asked for their help in setting up the recording equipment. They were impressed by our modern, compact recorders and seemed to enjoy wearing the lapel microphones we provided. One child said it was a bit like 'talking on TV, only a bit better than talking on TV'. We tested the equipment by asking some questions and playing back their answers. The questions gave the children opportunities to practise their interviewee roles..

At this point, we suggested that the children rehearse not answering particular questions. Some children found it hard to imagine that they might want to do this. For instance, one girl said she would want to answer all the questions because 'I'm a good chatterer – my mother says I am'. Another explained, 'Probably I'll just answer all of them, 'cause I'm used to it'. Nevertheless, collectively the children thought of several ways of expressing this, including:

- Pass.
- No comment.
- Sorry, I just don't want to tell you that.

Similarly, some of the children took some convincing that they might want to take a break during the interview or end it themselves. One boy was adamant when he said, 'I'll want to go on, I'll want to go on,' and another protested, 'I do want to talk to you'. However, even these children eventually agreed to a way of communicating that they wanted to stop the interview, either temporarily or completely. They practised the following words and phrases:

- Stop.
- I've had enough.
- Please may we stop now?
- I don't want to talk anymore.
- Do you mind if I have a rest from talking?
- Sorry, I'm getting bored.

One of the girls preferred to put up her hand instead of using words.

We also offered reassurance that what the children said would not be repeated to their adoptive parents, their teachers, or anyone else they knew. However, we pointed out that *they* could tell other people about the interview.

This aspect of confidentiality made the start of one of the younger girl's interviews particularly difficult. Her brother had been interviewed immediately before her and she was distracted by her desperation to know what he had said and done during his interview. The interviewer explained that she was not able to discuss his interview with her, but suggested that she could ask him if he was willing to talk about it later.

We also stressed that the questions were not a test. Before going any further we went through a simple consent form with them and asked if they were happy to sign it (see Appendix H).

Some children clearly appreciated being given the opportunity to influence some aspects of the interview. They exercised their right not to answer certain questions in exactly the way they had practised. An eight-year-old elaborated a little when she felt she could not answer a question about how her therapist was helpful:

> She helps me in all sorts of ways I can't really talk about. I'm not allowed to talk about what she tells me.

Others did not want certain parts of the interview recorded. Two children stopped the interview – one towards the end and the other made it clear at the start of the interview that she only wanted to talk for 25 minutes.

Family and friends

We then suggested that the children create what other researchers and practitioners have called "eco maps"[3] (see Appendix I). Essentially these were annotated pictures of the children's families, friends, and some of the professionals involved in their lives, including social workers and teachers. They illustrated the relationships between the children and others and provided an easy reference tool to help the interviewer personalise the rest of the interview. More particularly, the pictures helped them to find out who the children regarded as helpful and supportive.

There were several ways of completing a picture – the children could draw freehand, make lists, or use the project's "Smiles" stickers. Half the children chose to use the project stickers, 15 drew and six made lists. The picture or list was sometimes added to later in the interviews when the children remembered people they had previously forgotten. As the children

---

3   See Hill, Laybourn & Borland (1996).

created the pictures, they were encouraged to talk about their adoptive and birth parents; their siblings including full, half, foster and adoptive brothers and sisters; extended family members; friends; and professionals. Most children seemed at ease with the inclusion of their birth families in the picture. Although some children had done similar exercises before with other professionals, this did not seem to affect their enthusiasm for the exercise.

Main questions and themes

During the third stage of the interview we sought to explore the children's subjective experiences of the adoption process, focusing on the help they received during that process. Our agenda was carefully balanced with theirs. A checklist or tightly structured questionnaire would not have been appropriate. We were aware from the parental interviews that the children had different placement histories. We therefore developed a framework for inquiry and discussion which identified the topics we wanted to cover. In addition to asking the participants the questions within the framework that were relevant to them, we asked supplementary questions, beyond the common framework, following each child's personal experience and line of thinking.

In anticipation of some children finding it difficult to 'just talk' about such potentially difficult times in their lives, we developed some materials that would make communication easier. A graphic designer created some pictorial prompt cards (see Appendix J). These represented the different stages of the adoption process and provided starting points for exploring the children's views and experiences.

These cards encouraged the children to think of the adoption process as a journey and represented the stages on that journey. They were joined together to form a road in what ever order the children chose. If the children identified other stages they were encouraged to make new cards.

The cards were offered to the children at the discretion of the interviewer. Twelve children were offered the cards and two of them declined to use them. The cards were used in a variety of ways. For example, they helped some children through the whole of the main section of the interview. For others they served simply to get the interview going or at the end to return to topics for further exploration.

During the interviews, a few of the children talked about problems of which other people were apparently unaware. These centred around bullying at school and the desire to be in contact with or know more about members of their birth families from whom they were separated. In these instances, we responded by carefully exploring whether the children wanted to share these anxieties with anyone else and, if so, gently encouraged them to do so. It seemed as though once they had articulated the problem during the interview they were then quite keen to talk about it with somebody else. In fact they all decided to try to discuss their concerns with their adoptive parents or social workers. We also had information to give to the children about other sources of help, including ChildLine and the NSPCC, although the need for it did not arise.

Ending the interview

We thanked the children for helping and offered them a certificate (see Appendix K) for taking part in the study. We had wondered whether the certificates would appeal to the older children in the sample, but in fact all the participants seemed very pleased to accept them.

As we packed away the resources, some of the children asked to play back some of the tape-recording again and enjoyed hearing their own voices. While they listened we took another opportunity to reassure them that their tapes would be kept safe.

A personalised thank you card was also posted to the children at a later date.

DATA ANALYSIS

In view of our essentially qualitative approach, all the interviews were different in their structure and content. As already noted, it was rare for a child to cover all topics. To analyse the material, the interviews were transcribed in full and then systematically broken down into frames of text. A coding system was developed and used with the help of the software, NuD.ist, to group together text containing similar ideas, perceptions, issues and themes.

In reporting our findings we have only presented selected fragments of the interview transcripts. To reassure the reader that we have, nevertheless, surveyed the whole body of data, we have included some simple figures – frequencies and percentages – and cited some unusual cases (see Silverman,

1993, p.162). We have quoted directly from 40 of the 41 interviews. We have used names for readability. However, all names and place names have been changed to disguise the children's identities. Names have also been interchanged to ensure that one child's comment cannot be followed throughout the report. Other slight changes in detail have been made specifically to preserve the children's anonymity.

In addition, we recognised the importance of issues of "race" and ethnicity within the adoption process, particularly in the light of more than two decades of concern about the numbers of black children in care and the debate about transracial versus same-race placements. In reporting our findings that are relevant to these issues, we have chosen not to write a separate chapter, but integrate them into all chapters as in the *Supporting Adoption* study (Lowe and Murch, 1999, p.4).

3 The Beginning of the Process

INTRODUCTION

In this section we report the children's views and experiences of what we regarded for the purposes of this study to be the beginning of the adoption process: the time adoption was first suggested to the children. We aimed to explore their subjective experience of any pre-placement preparatory work they had undertaken which introduced them to the idea of a new adoptive family; helped them to express their wishes, feelings and hopes about it; and explained the rest of the adoption process. We also wanted to find out whether and in what ways they valued this work. However, for reasons explained below, we found this to be the most difficult part of the children's experience of the adoption process to explore and the data reported here are not as rich as we had hoped.

We had problems preparing key questions given the nebulous nature of preparation for adoption. First, preparatory work is difficult to isolate from other pre-placement direct work with children. It may be a part of life story work which, as Triseliotis *et al* (1997) explain, aims to help children deal with painful and traumatic memories from the past; unravel confusion, build self-esteem and a positive sense of identity; and understand the reasons for moves. Sometimes it may in fact be called "life story work", but it is not necessarily given a label at all. It may also be similar to other direct work children may have done with social workers and other professionals earlier in their lives. Secondly, preparation is undertaken by different people. Some of it is done by the children's social workers, but other professionals such as child therapists and play workers can also be involved, as well as the children's carers. Thirdly, practitioners use different tools and techniques for this work depending on the individual needs of children, their own training, and time and resources available. Often it can involve no more than talking. It may, however, centre around the creation of a life story book or include alternative methods, such as play or the exploration of dreams.[1] Being aware

---

1   See Cipolla, Benson McGown & Yanulis (1992) and Harper (1996).

of all these possible experiences, we therefore planned simply to ask the children who had first talked to them about adoption and explore what was said, particularly about the meaning of the concept and the rest of the process. We then intended to ask what they felt about the idea at the time and whether they had found their early preparation helpful, adjusting our questions to whatever form it had taken.

We also had difficulties because the children found it hard to remember the beginning of the process. Often they only had vague memories of being introduced to the idea. Even those who could recall something about it were much more hesitant in their answers than, for example, when responding to questions about their current relationships, their more recent experiences, and the more easily defined and discrete parts of the process. We tried to help by encouraging them to think back to the relevant time and place, but if they continued to struggle to remember, we felt it better to move on to another stage of the process.

FINDINGS

Being introduced to the idea of adoption

By social workers

Overall, 33 of the children were asked about the beginning of the process and a third of this sub-sample suggested that their social workers were the first to broach the subject. Janine, who was 14 years old when she was interviewed, thought it was her social worker who spoke to her about it for the first time when she was living in a Community Home. She explained:

> I remember having to go to the court a couple of times, which was quite upsetting. And then I remember being told that I wouldn't be going back to live with my Mum, because they didn't feel it was safe or right.

She said she did not know what adoption meant at first, but reflected:

> I think they had to tell me that I wouldn't be going home first and that I would be moving to live with someone else permanently, who would be my parents.

Janine mentioned that she had thought about discussing it with other girls in the Community Home who were in the same position, but said she had not done so. She explained:

> *This was happening to them and they needed to worry about themselves and their family.*

David (aged 12) also remembered initially talking about adoption with his social worker, and similarly did not discuss it with anybody else, not even his foster carers. At first he said he did not understand and asked his social worker many questions.

David	*He had to explain it to me a couple of times and then I had my queries . . . It took me quite a while. And I kept asking questions all over again and he answered them.*
Interviewer	*Can you remember any of the questions you asked him?*
David	*How long will I be with my Mum and Dad? . . . I can't remember what the other questions were.*

Although David could not recall what else he wanted to know at this stage, he was positive about this social work support. He said:

> He [social worker] *kept explaining it to me and he kept asking me if I understood.*

Similarly, Melanie (aged 10) recalled discussing adoption only with her social worker. She explained that she never really had time to speak to her foster carers because they had several other children to look after. However, when asked whether she had wanted to speak to anybody else, she replied, 'No, I was OK'.

By foster carers

Four of the sub-sample remembered members of their foster families being the first people to raise the possibility of adoption. For instance, Peter (aged 11), whose foster placement developed into an adoptive one, said:

> *I think I was about eight when it came up, because I didn't know what the word meant when I was six or seven.*

Evidently his foster carers had to explain it many times and told him, 'it's totally up to you'. He also remembered discussing it with members of his foster carers' extended family and receiving additional explanations from them.

Andy (aged 11) also recalled that his foster carers were the first to talk to him about adoption. He said: 'I didn't know what it meant then, but I do now'. He also spoke to his foster brother while using their computer. If they were playing games they might 'just start talking' about adoption. Although Andy could not remember what his foster brother had said, he had confidence in his views because his brother was himself adopted.

By social workers and foster carers

Eight children said they had spoken to both social workers and foster carers about adoption at the beginning of the process. Mandy (aged 11) elaborated; unusually within our sample, she was still living with her birth mother when a social worker first told her that she was to be adopted. She recalled that the 'Head of the Social Workers' had helped her birth mother to look after her for a few days because her birth mother 'wasn't looking after me properly'. The 'Head of Social Workers' then decided that she was to be adopted because 'she didn't think it was a good home'. Mandy was then helped to prepare for adoption by another social worker who, according to her, also thought adoption was a very good idea. She remembered her foster mother being involved as well. She said:

Mandy   *I wasn't quite sure what adoption actually meant, but I knew it was a place where I would stay and be looked after.*

Interviewer   *Did anyone explain to you what it meant?*

Mandy   *My foster mother just said that, 'You'll be safe with these people,' and she said, 'I'll visit you sometimes, so there's no need to worry'. My foster mother told us what adoption meant 'cause she was my last foster parent . . . She told me not to worry and that she'd be sad that I'd go, but she'd know that I would have a nice time there and that I'd grow up to be good and healthy and stuff like that.*

It was easy for Wanda (aged 12) to remember who had been involved in her preparation, but it was hard for her to remember exactly what was said. This was hardly surprising because her preparation had begun at least five years earlier.

Wanda   *I think it was . . . [my foster parents] and my social worker who was called Amy. They, at the same time, talked to me about what adoption was and what I would do, what I had to do.*

Interviewer   *Do you remember what sorts of things they explained?*

Wanda   *They got in touch with this Mum . . . and they explained with my Mum, what kinds of things would happen.*

Interviewer   *So do you remember what they said would happen?*

Wanda   [Hesitantly] *They said – not really, no.* [Laughing]

Interviewer   *It's going back a long way. It's a long time ago, isn't it?*

Wanda   *They said that I would have to go to court . . .*

She also remembered talking to her foster carers' children who had been adopted, '. . . so they told me what it was like for them'. When asked what the children told her, Wanda mentioned court again. She said the children told her they had to go to court.

Debbie (aged 10) was the only child in the sample who mentioned taking part in a meeting about her adoption. We do not know what efforts were made by the professionals to facilitate her participation,[2] but Debbie did not seem to find it a valuable experience. She said:

> *We had a meeting with foster parents. We had a meeting with [my siblings] and their social workers and my social worker about adoption . . . [My siblings] and I wanted to go off and play, because it got a bit boring after a while.*

By others

More unusually, when Lucy (aged 10) was asked who first talked to her about adoption she said she thought it was her judge. Mark (aged 11) could also have been thinking of a judge when he answered the same question

---

2   See Schemmings (1996).

saying, 'The man who was doing our adoption . . . he was in the Law Court place'. Thomas (aged 9) also gave an unusual answer to the question. He replied, 'I can remember, I think it was a man, but I don't remember who'. He then recalled:

> I had to post boxes . . . They're like this box and you have all these different cards that you're posting and he, like he asks you questions and you put in the one you think is best for it.[3]

His mother, who was present during the interview, then explained that at the very beginning of the process Thomas had been to see a child psychologist. When asked exploratory questions, however, Thomas did not recall any other details of this work.

As part of life story work

Eleven children connected first talking about adoption with their life story work.[4] For instance, Nicky (aged 11) recalled that her social workers, including Joan and Bob, were the first people to talk to her about adoption while they were doing her life story book.

Nicky   *Joan did a bit. Bob didn't talk to us much about it because he was trying to find us a home and he was like talking to Mum and Dad. But he was nice to us , but we didn't really talk about the past with him. It was more Joan and the social worker before . . . We used to go to this big office and do drawing and everything. I've got a Life Book . . . and the other lady, I've forgotten her name, she used to do that as well. Used to draw and write things.*

Interviewer   *Did you find that helpful?*

Nicky   *Yeah, at the time . . . A little bit.*

Interviewer   *A little bit?*

---

3   Thomas was perhaps referring to the Benny & Anthony psychometric test for systematically recording and quantifying children's feelings about their family relationships.

4   Overall 33 children had life story books. Sixteen of them made it clear that they had completed the work before moving to their adoptive placements; four began after they were placed; but it was not possible to clarify the timing of the work for 13 of them.

Nicky	Not a lot, but I started to know what adoption means. That's it really.

Life story work also seemed to be an integral part of 12-year-old Ian's early preparation. His comments suggested that, during this stage of the process, he talked about both the past and the future with his social worker.

> Well, sometimes it was difficult because we didn't know what was happening and she told us what's happening and then we got used to it, and then she said, 'Is there anything else you would like to tell me?' . . . She told us a lot of things about what had happened that we didn't know.

Although Ian could not remember the detail, he was, nevertheless, positive about this social worker, saying:

Ian	Sometimes we used to do things with them and talk to them a lot. Loads of things.
Interviewer	Was that helpful?
Ian	Yeah. Sometimes they used to take us out and talk about it and what's happened and tell us the news. Loads of things they used to tell us. Can't remember them all though.

Simon (aged 14) recalled first discussing adoption with his Community Home key-workers, Hazel and Carol, whom he called 'my helpers'. He thought they did not explain what it meant until he was a little older, seven or eight, because they said he would not understand. He added that they were just talking about his family when he was younger and described this work in the following way:

Simon	About every so often . . . I had an afternoon off school and Hazel used to come and talk to me. I had a family train with everyone on it in my family. We used to look through magazines to put a background on it as well . . . It was a Thomas the Tank Engine . . . Just a paper one, pinned up on a board.

Interviewer	And the train represented your family?
Simon	You had to cut out people and put them in.
Interviewer	And then did she ask you about the people in your family?
Simon	Sometimes. Once she took me to where she worked, in the office, and there was this house and it had a sand-pit and you used to put candles to represent all the people in your family and you could draw roads and stuff in the sand and houses, put different people in the different houses, and that was fun because I was only five then.

Although he said the train was kept by the key-workers for the other children, he valued his memories of this work. He did not recall discussing adoption with anyone other than Hazel and Carol. However, he found talking about it with them helpful, reflecting:

> If they didn't talk I wouldn't have known what was going on . . .
> They said it was better that I understood what was going on.

Riahanna (age 12) said it was either her foster carers who raised the issue of adoption or 'a lady who came and did a group with us, with our folders'. When asked if she could tell the interviewer a little more about this lady and her folder, Riahanna said:

> She was with us when we were in the Children's Home and she
> . . . no, no, she came and spoke to us all individually and said
> what we thought about not living with our parents and what's
> happened and we used to talk to her about it. And then we went
> on to folders and doing work with her and different things about
> the past and what we were doing at the present time and things
> like that.

Riahanna said she sometimes found this helpful, but not at other times. She explained that sometimes she did not value it because she did not believe she would be adopted. At other times she appreciated being helped to 'do something for the future'.

Despite this preparatory work, Riahanna also said she still felt panicky and was left wondering what was going to happen. She was also left feeling as though she were:

> In a little dream thinking ... you were never gonna move on and
> the process was a bit slow. But on the other hand it kinda went
> quick if you didn't think about it a lot ... A bit of a dream. Adrift.

Early wishes and feelings about adoption

Thirty-two of the children were asked about their early wishes and feelings
about the notion of adoption. Equal numbers of children remembered
feeling broadly positive and negative, eight and nine respectively. Almost as
many had complicated and contradictory feelings, and two children
suggested that at that time they were young and did not really understand
and consequently just went along with it and did as they were told. Another
seven children simply did not know or could not remember what they felt
about adoption when it was first suggested.

Most of the children who remembered feeling positive about adoption
were in foster placements which became their adoptive placements. For
instance, Kirsty (aged 8), one of the youngest children in the sample, who
called her foster carer "Nanny" said:

> I decided it myself ... I just wanted to stay here. And Nanny said,
> 'Do you?' and Nanny said, 'We want to be adopted'.

Kirsty may have mistakenly recalled Nanny saying, 'We want to be adopted'.
However, she could also have been acknowledging that adoption is a two-
way process and that she and her adoptive mother had wanted to adopt
each other.

Similarly, Anna (aged 14) suggested that the decision to be adopted
had very much been her own.

Anna	*I was fostered for two years and then I decided I wanted to get adopted and ...*
Interviewer	[Interrupting] *You decided?*
Anna	*Yeah. And then I was allowed to have the decision whether or not to get adopted ... I really wanted to be adopted. Mum and Dad said it was up to me.*

Jocelyn (aged 12) said her social worker had given her the idea and then she asked her foster mother. She explained that she wanted her foster mother to adopt her because she felt all her previous foster carers had been horrible to her. She added, 'It meant quite a lot, because that meant I could stay with my Mum when I wanted to'.

Mark thought adoption was a good idea because, 'my Mum and Dad were better and would look after me more'. When asked in what way his foster carers were better, he replied, 'They could feed me, and clothes and stuff, because my Mum couldn't do that'.

Several children were not keen on adoption at first, because, as Justin (aged 9) explained, 'I didn't know what my family would be like'. Judy (aged 11) said that this particular uncertainty made her feel scared and worried about the idea. Despite knowing his foster carers who wanted to adopt him, Mike (aged 9) still had reservations. He said he did not think it was going to work out well because in his view he had not been placed with the family for long enough. When Fiona (aged 9) was asked what she thought of the idea she said, very sadly:

> I didn't want to move. I wanted to stay with [my foster parents],
> 'cause I'd been moved around so much.

Some of the children expressed contradictory wishes and feelings. Melanie, for instance, said, 'I thought it was okay, but I was sad to leave my Mum'.

Mary (aged 9) remembered wanting to stay with her current foster carer and that she 'didn't wanna go with nobody else'. She also thought, however, that having 'new' parents was preferable to returning to previous foster carers.

Although Chantelle (aged 9) wanted to be adopted, she was also troubled by the concept.

Chantelle   *I was quite surprised actually.*

Interviewer   *Did you think it was the right thing?*

Chantelle   *Yes.* [Emphatically]

Interviewer   *Why were you surprised?*

Chantelle   *Any child would be surprised if they knew their parents*
              were going to give you to someone else. Any child
              would be surprised.

Eighteen children were asked if they had had a chance to tell anybody what they felt about adoption at this early stage. Ten of them said 'no', that they 'didn't know', 'couldn't remember', or referred to being asked later in the process. Andy and Mark, for instance, mentioned their judges asking them if they wanted to be adopted. Chantelle was quite clear that she had not been asked at this stage. She said, 'No. And when I came here, that's the only time I was asked,' and suggested that she felt under some pressure to accept her placement: 'If I didn't want to I would have gone through the process again and again and again'.

The other eight children had been asked what they felt about the idea of adoption by social workers, foster carers and other children. Janine remembered being asked on several occasions by social workers and said her answer was always that she did not want to be adopted. She added that when her adoption subsequently went ahead she wondered why they had bothered to asked her. She felt her view did not actually count.

SUMMARY

The main points from the children's views and experiences of being introduced to the idea of adoption are:

- Some children remembered rather hazily that they were introduced to the idea of adoption by social workers, foster carers, or both. They recalled that at first they found it a difficult concept to understand and they needed repeated explanations.
- When the idea of adoption was introduced, it was more acceptable to children whose prospective adoptive parents were their foster carers, than to those who were going to have to leave their foster carers and be adopted by strangers.

4 Matching and Introductions

INTRODUCTION

After children have been introduced to the idea of adoption, they experience a period of waiting before they are matched with prospective adoptive families. The length of this waiting time varies according to how easy or difficult it is for social workers to find new families for them which meet their needs. The children, therefore, have to live for unpredictable lengths of time with the uncertainty of whether or not suitable families will be found.

During this waiting time the children may be directly involved in the adoption agency workers' assessment of their needs. They may also begin or continue life story and other preparatory work with their social workers. As we noted in Chapter 3, such work aims to help children establish an accurate picture of their birth families and complex pasts, and to prepare them for separation from their current carers and the move to a new home with a minimum of confusion and anxiety. The level of social work visiting during this waiting period, however, may vary from case to case and over time. Foster carers may contribute to the preparation process, less formally, as part of everyday life, through talking to the children about future plans and encouraging a positive view of the move (Rushton et al, 1998).

Another stage in the matching process is the linking of children and families. Again practice varies from case to case. According to the *Supporting Adoption* study,[1] for the agency workers involved, current considerations for linking are geography; finance; inter-agency contracts; children's needs; adopters' needs; the involvement of birth parents in choosing adopters; and ethnicity (meaning the religion, "race", culture and language of children and adopters). Those for adopters are children's special needs; children's ages; children's wishes and feelings; and ethnicity. The progress of linking may also be affected by a number of factors including the needs and age of the child; more than one couple or single parent being considered as adopters; and adopters having doubts about proceeding with the match.

---

1   See *Supporting Adoption* (Lowe and Murch, 1999), Chapter 10, Issues in Matching, para. 3, p.161–169.

The *Supporting Adoption*[2] study describes how once a link has been made, the process of matching continues to vary. One possible sequence of events is for the child's social worker and adopters' social worker to attend an adoption panel meeting where the suitability of a link is considered. Then the prospective adopters' social worker may contact the prospective adopters with a brief description of the child or children. If they are interested, the child's social worker may visit the parents, giving them more information to help them decide whether to proceed. The children may participate in the preparation of some of the information produced for this purpose.

The next stage for the prospective adopters, according to the *Supporting Adoption* study,[3] may be a sighting of the child from a distance, unbeknown to the child. Alternatively the children may be involved in making a video of themselves so that would-be adopters can get a sense of them without the necessity of a meeting. A plan for the children and prospective parents to meet and begin to get to know each other may then be made. In preparation for a meeting, the children may be given verbal, written and photographic information about their would-be parents.

During the introductory period, adopters may become more involved with the child's social worker and carers, and may meet other professionals who are helping the child in some way. As introductions progress, the children are usually taken out by the adopters, first for a few hours and then for a day. They then may begin to visit the adopters' home, eventually staying overnight and for weekends. Some telephone each other between visits. The progress of introductions is monitored by the agency. Sometimes the children or their prospective parents have doubts about the match and, if they cannot be resolved, the children may be helped to see that a different match may work better. Alternatively, it may be possible to work through the uncertainty. Finally, a time is agreed for the placement of the child with the adoptive family (Fahlberg, 1994).

The variation in practice made the formulation of key questions for matching challenging. As with our questions about the beginning of the adoption process, to make them relevant to as many of the sample as possible, we kept them broad. We began by asking them if they

---

2   See *Supporting Adoption* (Lowe and Murch, 1999), Chapter 10, Issues in Matching.
3   See *Supporting Adoption* (Lowe and Murch, 1999), Chapter 10, Issues in Matching, para. 4.2.

remembered what kind of family they wanted. We then asked about their views and experiences of the waiting periods before being matched with new families; receiving information about their prospective families; providing information about themselves for their would-be parents; and meeting and beginning to get to know their adopters.

When reading the findings reported in this chapter, it is important to bear in mind that, in researching matching, we were once again hampered by the retrospective nature of the study and the understandable difficulties children have in recalling events which happened some time ago and when some of them were quite young.

FINDINGS

The adoptive families the children wanted

Seventeen of the children told us what kind of family they wanted. Five of the children clearly remembered wanting new families which included other children. They explained this in terms of not wanting to be on their own for fear of being bored and liking to be around lots of people. Only one child recalled being keen to begin his new family life as an only child. He explained that he believed he could 'get to know whoever it was better . . . because I think it's easier to know someone if you're alone'. Another child, however, remembered having more contradictory feelings. At times she wanted a family without siblings and saw this as a way of securing more attention for herself. At other times she was very keen to remain living with her birth sister from whom she had already been separated and reunited.

Five children remembered clearly wanting to be placed with their birth siblings. Ultimately four of them were placed on their own or with just one sibling and one child remained with her brother and sister as she wished. Anna (aged 14) explained that she was keen to stay in a long-term placement with two of her siblings, but was eventually separated from them. She understood the decision in the following way:

> [My foster mother] *couldn't cope and she didn't have the room. And she thought it would be better off for me if I, sort of, had time and had a family of my own that could actually look after me . . . It was upsetting, but we managed to get over it. [My siblings]* were very upset. We kept in contact . . .

Almost in tears, Judy (aged 11) recalled that she had wanted to be placed with her sister and said it was very upsetting to be separated. She explained in a whisper:

> Well, she was my half-sister and my first – I've had two social workers – my first social worker thought it would be better if I was on my own. So we just had to be separated.

Nicky (aged 11) also remembered this issue being discussed. Although she acknowledged that she did not always get on well with her siblings, she 'wanted them both because we were going to get split up, yeah, but we stayed together'.

By contrast, one girl (aged 12) was adamant that she did not want to be placed with her siblings who she felt were always horrible to her. She remembered talking about the option of a group placement with her social workers and was glad this did not happen. Just two of the children recalled discussing with their social workers the possibility of having a single parent. One of them, who was eventually placed with a married couple, remembered that he had only wanted a father, imagining that he would be able to mess around a bit more with a father rather than a mother.

Another girl (aged 12), who was placed with a single woman, said her social workers had decided that 'a single parent, a female . . . my adoptive Mum, would be best for me'. She said:

> There were some bigger families, with four people already there, brother, sister, Mum, Dad, people like that. They were mixed people and I wasn't sure what people I would like to have lived with.

She then added that she did not mind really not having a father and siblings, but let her social workers know that what was more important to her was that her new family should include a cat.

Collectively the children wanted parents who were 'nice', 'kind', 'funny' and 'normal'. More particularly, Debbie (aged 10) wanted hers to be fun and active. David (aged 12) wished for parents in their 30s and for a father with whom he could go camping. Five of the children, perhaps with their experiences of neglect and ill treatment in mind, mentioned wanting parents who would care for them well. Mandy (aged 11) said:

> I wanted somebody to look after and love me and do all that kind of stuff and basically look after me and bring me up properly.

> *Someone who will look after me if I'm hurt and sad and someone who will play with me.*

Another girl (aged 8) said:

> *I wanted a family that would take care of me and not leave me alone. And when I want them, they always come. And feed me properly, and look after me, and be kind . . .*

Ian (aged 12) explained that he wanted his new family to help him and his siblings get over their difficult past experiences. One of his sisters mentioned that, not only did she wish for parents who would give her the freedom to wear make-up, but she also wanted a mother and father who 'didn't smack'.

Three of the girls spoke about the physical characteristics of their desired parents. One (aged 11) said she wanted 'a Mum with long hair so I could play with it and a Dad without a moustache'. She added, laughing, 'But I got a Mum with short hair and a Dad with a moustache'. Chantelle (aged 9) explained that she had always wanted a big mummy so that she could cuddle up to her every night. Judy described the parents she imagined when her social worker told her she had found parents that would suit her. She said, 'I thought that meant they'd look like me and have blue eyes, have fair hair, because I have . . .'

Waiting to be matched with an adoptive family

It was understandably difficult for most of the children to recall the exact lengths of time between being introduced to the idea of adoption and being matched with a new family. Andy (aged 11), who used the pictorial prompt cards during his interview, described his wait in the following terms.

Interviewer	*Somewhere in this pack of cards I've got some cards about waiting.*
Andy	*I did a lot of that!*
Interviewer	*Would you like to choose a card to join up the roads for waiting?*
Andy	*Well, start, then wait, wait, wait and once more, then wait.*

Interviewer	Do you remember how long you had to wait for your new family?
Andy	Ages! And then go a bit further, then wait, and we've run out of waiting cards!

Seventeen of the sample nevertheless told us something about their experience of waiting. Half this sub-sample said they had to wait too long while most of the other children were not sure if the waiting periods felt too long or too short. Just two sisters thought their family was found for them quickly.

Two children estimated waiting five years. Simon (aged 14) related his wait to his stay in a community home and explained:

> I was three when I first went in there, I was eight when I came out. So I had a long wait . . . I didn't like it. I think I had to wait too long.

One girl also said she had had to wait five years. When she was asked what the waiting was like she answered:

Girl	Terrible!
Interviewer	Terrible? What was terrible about it?
Girl	I wait, I wait, I wait, I wait . . .
Interviewer	Yes.
Girl	I wait for the telephone to ring every day . . .
Interviewer	And no news?
Girl	No news . . . until my fifth year.

Being advertised for adoption

Janine (aged 13) remembered being told by social workers that they were looking for an adoptive family for her whilst she was in a 'Children's Home' and subsequently spent at least two years with foster carers before moving to her adoptive home. During that time she was aware of being advertised for adoption in a catalogue or magazine and commented, in relation to her wait, that 'it didn't feel very nice, that you weren't being chosen'.

While waiting, other children in the sample were also aware of being advertised. Some were questioned about this, but another girl raised this as an issue without being prompted, saying that she was put in an adoption magazine paper. She said she was 'excited about seeing my picture in the paper. I remember going to take the picture, pulling all these weird faces'. Evidently a social worker who knew her 'quite well' wrote the text for the advertisement. The girl saw it after it was published and reflected:

> *I suppose she had to, but . . . I remember being angry when they said I was a moody child at times, that I could swing moods. I can remember being quite frustrated at that bit . . .*

One of the boys also remembered having his photograph taken and that, 'some people came over and took details off us . . . ' for the advertisement. His only comment about what was written was, 'they said [my brother] doesn't like crisps and he likes them'. When the boy was told how many families had responded to his advertisement he felt he and his brother were in demand. Laughing, he said he thought, 'it was good 'cause then we had quite a big chance of having some new parents'. Similarly, the girl remembered feeling amazed when she was told that several families had enquired about her.

Help with waiting to be matched with an adoptive family
The children explained what helped them through these waiting periods. Jocelyn's long wait was made more difficult by her anticipation of being newly separated from her birth siblings. She said she thought she would never see them again. She appreciated the reassurances her foster carers gave her that she would in fact be able to see them in their new homes. She also found social workers supportive and said everyone tried to help. Wanda similarly found her foster family and social worker helpful. She remembered:

> *They took me out to places so I'd forget about* [my adoption]. *Well, not forget, but I would also . . . have time with them before I went . . .*

Another girl's personal strategy was to try to forget about adoption and, she added:

> *If I was feeling down I'd speak to my friends . . . Speaking with* [my school friend] *and getting on with life as usual, that's usually the best way to cope with things.*

She added that she found it hard to 'wait for someone else to choose you out of a lot of other children'.

Other children also mentioned that making friends and playing with toys and foster siblings helped the time pass.

Being matched with new families

Two children recalled the exact moments they were told new families had been found for them. One remembered an unexpected visit from his social worker:

> I was brought home from school by someone and [my social worker] was at the Children's Home . . . If [my social worker] was there not on a Thursday I thought I might be in trouble. And they said, 'Well, you're gonna be adopted by these people,' and they showed me the video and the book, and I was really excited.

Another boy (aged 12) explained that he is often reminded of the moment he learnt that a new family had been found for him:

> I can remember that night when [my social worker] came over and we were all watching telly and then [my social worker] said, 'I've found a new Mummy and Daddy for you'. And I don't know why, but I burst into tears . . . I think it was the shock really. And at that time I didn't really want to leave [my foster mother]. And they didn't know what was wrong with me really. And I don't know why, but it's a reminder . . . when she said that she'd found a new Mum and Dad for me it was a Toys 'R' Us advert on telly. So now whenever I hear that Toys 'R' Us advert I always remember that night.

What the children wanted to know about their prospective families before they met them

Fourteen of the sample children were asked what they wanted to know about their new families before they met them. Understandably some of their questions were closely related to their wishes and feelings about the kinds of families they wanted. For instance, in addition to wanting to know about her new parents' personalities, Judy, who had wanted parents who looked like her, wanted to know whether they were tall and what colour hair they had. Another girl who wanted active parents was keen to know if hers were good fun and would be able to play football with her. One of the girls, who wanted parents who would care for her well, said she asked many questions. She explained: 'There's quite a lot we needed to know'. In particular she remembered asking: 'Am I going to have a good life and are they going to look after me properly?'

Four of the older children also remembered being curious about many aspects of their new parents' lives. When Jocelyn was asked what sorts of things she wanted to know about her new mother and father, she answered without hesitation, 'Everything!'. She went on to explain:

> What they were like? How old they were? What were their hobbies? What did they like doing? What didn't they like doing? What kind of children they'd like; boy or girl? Everything.

The two older boys also wanted to know about their prospective parents' jobs. Other children were particularly interested in their new houses and gardens.

Information the children received about their prospective families before they met them

Twenty-two of the children were asked questions about how and what they found out about their new families before they met them. Three of the children could not remember being told anything. For instance, Debbie was asked if she knew anything about her parents before she met them. She replied, 'No, they didn't tell me . . . ' Remembering her puzzlement at the time, she added, 'When I met them, they just said "Hello" to me, and I wondered who they were'. Three others recalled their social workers talking to them about their prospective parents. Judy remembered her social worker told her: 'They're very nice parents and they'll suit you and I know they'll look after you and love you'. She commented that she was 'very pleased to hear that, because it's good to have good parents'.

Two girls mentioned that they sometimes found it difficult to find the right words for their questions about their new family and also some of the information they received from social workers was confusing. One of them (aged 8) explained that, 'sometimes they didn't really say "Yes" or "No", and some of the questions were a bit difficult to say properly'. She added that occasionally 'even they' did not seem to know the answers to their questions.

Fourteen of the children said they were given books, videos, or both, by their new families prior to meeting them, or at their first meetings. Some of the children were a little unsure exactly when they were given to them. Their estimates ranged from a few months before their first meetings to the first meetings themselves.

The information given varied in content and style from family to family, but collectively the books included text, usually hand-written, and photographs of:

- prospective adoptive parents and siblings;
- family homes, inside and outside, including views from windows;
- gardens;
- family pets;
- the extended family;
- family friends;
- families celebrating special occasions;
- families engaged in their hobbies;
- a map of Britain showing the relationship between the children's current home and their prospective home; and
- local leisure facilities such as leisure centres, parks, shops, annual fairs, city farms and so on.

The videos were more detailed, covering fewer but similar aspects of their new families' lives. One boy gave the following description:

> And they started off over by the Green and then were taking [the dog] for a walk and then they came back to the house, showed me my room, then they went to show me my school, 200 yards up the road . . .

Another video included shots of their parents' house, from which they were able to choose their bedrooms, and 'Daddy was juggling apples from the bottom of the garden like a clown . . . '

The books and videos were greatly appreciated by the children. They were judged to be 'enjoyable', 'good', 'really good' and 'helpful, yeah, because when we came it could all be just a mystery to us'. Jocelyn found it helpful to see what her family looked like and for the video to show 'what the personality was . . . ' At another point during the interviews we asked the children about their special belongings. Interestingly, David identified his parents' introductory book as one of his prized objects.

However, two children mentioned that they found it difficult to take the books and videos seriously. They had been waiting for adoptive parents for so long that they did not believe they would ever be found. When one girl saw her parents' video for the first time she did not feel the people and the house were real. Similarly by this stage, one of the boys had come to believe that adoption 'was just like a game that [social workers] played'.

Information about themselves for their prospective parents

Seventeen of the sample were asked questions concerning the information about themselves which was provided for their new families. A few replied that they did not know or had not thought about it, but others felt they wanted their prospective parents to know something about their needs, likes, dislikes and personal qualities.

One girl expressed a general appreciation of a need for her parents to know something about her, in advance of meeting them:

> I thought to myself that it wouldn't be much point having a
> family that doesn't know anything about you.

More particularly she wanted them to know:

> . . . what food I liked, what I liked playing, and that I liked Mickey
> Mouse a lot. And that I was quite a good girl.

Andy light-heartedly said that it was particularly important that his parents should know the date of his birthday. Evidently he wanted to be sure of receiving lots of presents. Jackie (aged 8) wanted her parents to know that she was 'cuddleable'.

One child said he felt it was vital for his parents to know what had happened to him and his brother in the past. He also mentioned that he and his brother had been matched with a prospective adoptive couple who later withdrew from the process. He understood that 'half-way through it they said they weren't suitable for us . . . ' when they learnt about their pasts and 'couldn't handle it'. Although this had been disappointing, he still felt that it was valuable for his future parents to have 'read some of the details . . . ' and to be able to accept them. Similar views may have been underlying another child's desire for her prospective parents to see her life story book.

We then tried to explore the children's awareness and views of the actual information that was communicated. Debbie thought her foster carers had met her new parents and told them 'little parts about me'. Ruth (aged 11) and Karen (aged 13) thought their parents had gone to see their social worker and were 'told a bit about us'. None of the children within this sample remembered making books for this purpose, although one of the girls had adopted sisters who had done so. Interestingly, Mandy (aged 11) said she was introduced to her prospective parents soon after they had seen a photograph of her. She therefore said she 'didn't think we had enough time to make a book or video'.

Just three children made videos. One boy made his with the help of his social worker and residential key-worker. He described it as being,

> . . . just like someone interviewing me . . . I was using one of my friend's computers at that moment and they were filming me as I was playing on it . . . They were just asking me what kind of computer games I was playing, stuff like that. Just chatting to me . . . There's some film of me there when I was swimming.

He judged the finished tape to be 'fine'. Two sisters were not sure who held the camera when their video was made, but remembered they were filmed playing with their foster family's pets in the garden. One of them was asked, 'What was it like having to make the video?'. After a long pause, she replied, 'I think it was fun really, because we were just doing what we wanted, what we like doing'.

First meetings with prospective adoptive families

Twenty-eight of the sample were asked about their first meetings with their adoptive families. Some of the children simply described what happened during the meeting – where they met, who was involved, and what they did – without judging it in any way. However, about twenty of them also expressed their feelings about it. Five talked about their meetings in positive terms, three remembered a mixture of positive and negative feelings, but the majority only recalled feeling varying degrees of shyness and fear about the experience.

Luke (aged 9) was one of the children who seemed unreservedly to enjoy their first meetings with their new families:

Interviewer   *Can you remember when you met your Mum and Dad?*

Luke   *This Mum and Dad? . . . Yeah!*

Interviewer   *What was it like?*

Luke   *Well it was very happy. I was very happy.*

Interviewer   *What were you happy about?*

Luke   *It's because I got a new Mum and Dad who were nice to me. [Pause]*

Interviewer   *What did you do the day that you met them? Did you go out together?*

Luke   *Yeah. I kept hugging them.*

One boy remembered that it was 'really nice' when he first met his prospective parents. He said they 'looked nice' and he thought, 'Brilliant, I'm going to go'. His brother also thought their meeting was good. He recalled talking with his new mother and father in his foster carers' living room for about three hours and receiving their introductory book. Afterwards he showed his new father his bedroom and played a computer game. He said, with a smile, 'Dad was hopeless at it'. He also mentioned, 'And when I came back to the foster home after the introduction at the weekend, I started crying 'cause I wanted to go back'.

The children who had more mixed feelings about their first meetings included Wanda and Judy. Wanda described feeling both shy and excited. Judy said:

> *I felt a bit – I was worried and that and scary and – I don't know [sighing]. I felt pleased that I'd found them, but I didn't know what they'd be like . . . And we had a meal together the first time . . . we went to the zoo and things and it was really fun.*

Another girl acknowledged that she often felt nervous and excited when meeting new people, in fact she felt it was instinctive. However, she went on to explain that this particular meeting was especially demanding:

> *I think you're so nervous about meeting the people because you know they've chosen you because they think you're better. I mean they've looked through a whole catalogue or magazine . . . and seen you and thought that's who they wanted. So you feel nervous about meeting them. You think, 'Well, am I going to be good enough?'.*

The majority of the other children only remembered finding their first meetings difficult. One said:

> *It was strange, because, like, I didn't really know them. I didn't know what to speak about and* [my adoptive sister] *had gone shyer so she was like hiding and* [my adoptive brother] *wouldn't say anything . . . My foster carers were having a conversation with my Mum and Dad and* [my brother and sister] *just sat there . . . and I didn't want to say anything . . . It was funny. It was odd.*

When Sue was asked what her first meeting was like, she replied:

> *Quite scary . . . Well I didn't know them and I didn't know what they were going to be like.*

Another child described his first meeting in the following way:

> *I was drawing in* [my foster carer's] *living room and I remember them, like, looking at me. I think we were all shy then because we kept on looking at each other and then looking the other way . . . Well, I felt shy anyway. I don't know whether they felt shy . . . We went to the park to get to know each other . . .*

Daniel recounted how he helped his recently adopted, younger brother, Jack, to cope with their first meeting. Jack felt so shy that he hid under the table. Daniel got under the table with him and was the first member of the family to whom Jack spoke. Later that day Jack showed Daniel his bedroom and they played football together in the garden.

One boy (aged 14) also reflected on meeting his younger adopted brothers for the first time at their foster carers' home.

> *There was just these shy little things that were hiding behind the*

*settee ... when you're meeting somebody new for the first time
you ... would be pretty shy, wouldn't you? So I understood,
really, how they felt.*

A few other children found the meetings troublesome for other reasons. For instance, one of the girls, who felt scared herself, recalled that her brother cried because he 'didn't want a new mum and dad'. Lucy who said she was unclear who she was being introduced to, described her experience as 'a little bit strange'.

Being visited by or visiting prospective adoptive families

Almost three-quarters of the children told us something about being visited by or visiting their prospective adoptive families, or both, prior to their moves. Janine, one of the oldest girls in the sample, described her experience in the following way:

*I remember we saw them, we met them and ... they came
around a couple of times, about twice. Then we came here once
and then we went out a couple of times. And then we started
staying one night and then the weekend, then maybe a week. I'm
not sure if we stayed a week or not and then really we moved in
...*

Other children remembered visiting their prospective family home, but had no recollection of staying overnight.

Two of the children recalled spending all their time getting to know their new family in or around their foster homes and did not have the opportunity to visit their new homes before they moved. They only saw photographs of their new houses prior to moving because their foster placements were considerable distances from their prospective adoptive homes. One of the boys differentiated his experience from that of his newly adopted sister:

Boy	*I wasn't really like* [my sister]. *Because it's near Manchester, Leeds. She was able to take a day in our house and, when she wanted to, she came to sleep over for a night and then came back and then gradually she stayed longer and longer, but ...*
Girl	*Once I slept here for two weeks, didn't I?*

Boy	And we went to watch Cinderella, remember?
Girl	Yeah.
Boy	And with me, because Leeds and Penzance are so far away . . . they kept on talking about it saying, 'You can go to Leeds if you want'. And then when I did go to Leeds I would just stay really . . .

From the children's descriptions of visiting and staying with their adoptive families, we gained insights into their understanding of the purpose of these visits. Lucy (aged 10) recalled some confusion about the reason for her visits. She said:

> I thought I was just going round to somebody's house to play and staying there for the night or something. But I didn't know what it meant. Then they said, then they were gonna see me again. And I go, 'Why?'. It's like I didn't understand.

Some saw these visits as chances to familiarise themselves with their future home environment. They thought their visits were to see what the house was like and, as Mandy put it, 'I think the night here was so that we got used to our beds and the house and where things are'. Others talked in terms of opportunities for getting to know their new families. Debbie, who was placed with birth siblings from whom she had been separated, saw staying with the family as a chance to see what it felt like to live with her siblings again.

Those who were asked whether they found these visits helpful usually evaluated them positively in terms of chances to familiarise themselves with their new homes and families. For instance, Jocelyn said:

> It made it easier . . . 'Cause like I know my way around and knew where I stood and I knew where my room was. And I knew where everything was and it was easier . . .

Others, however, talked about some difficulties associated with the visits. Three remembered feeling a little bit upset and sad about being away from their foster families. Another three said they disliked the long car or coach journeys that the visits necessitated.

Ian appreciated having had the opportunity to express his and his siblings' wishes and feelings to professionals during this introductory period.

Ian   First we came here and had a look and then we went
               back and we chatted to the social worker. And we said,
               'Yes, we'd like to go there,' and all sorts of things. So
               then we went here. Packed all the bags and came. We
               were adopted.

Interviewer   What sorts of other things did you say? Can you
               remember?

Ian   I think so. Like, it's nice to be here. Sometimes I said it's
               nice and warm . . .

Sue also remembered being asked her wishes and feelings at this stage, but
found her social worker unhelpful.

Sue   She didn't want us to move in 'cause she kept on
               saying, 'Well, if you don't want to come here then you
               don't have to you know . . . No need to say Yes just
               because I want you to say . . . just because I said you
               had to say Yes or something or something like that. Like
               trying to make us change our mind . . . [pause]

Interviewer   So it sounded to you as though she didn't want you . . .

Sue   To come . . .

Interviewer   And what did you feel about that?

Sue   I don't know. I wanted to come here.

SUMMARY

The main points raised by the children about their views and experiences of
being matched with and introduced to a new family can be summarised as
follows:

- The children had ideas about the personal qualities, age, interests,
  parenting skills and physical attributes of the parents they
  wanted, as well as preferences for family size and composition.
- After being introduced to the idea of adoption, half (53 per cent)
  a sub-sample of 17 children had painfully long waiting periods

before they were matched with their new families. Some coped with waiting by trying to get on with their lives and making the most of their current relationships and situations. Others coped by discounting adoption as a serious possibility.

- When the children were matched with new families they wanted information about many aspects of their prospective parents' lives. Some of the information they wanted related to their ideas about the kinds of families they wanted. The children appreciated the books and videos they received, giving them information about their prospective parents. They found them to be very helpful.

- With a few exceptions, the children did not feel included in the preparation or presentation of information about themselves for their new families. The children wanted their prospective parents to know something about their needs, likes, dislikes and personal qualities. A few of the older children had wanted them to know about their troubled pasts. The few children who commented on the advertisements that were used to help find families for them had reservations about the ways in which the advertisements portrayed them.

- Being visited by and visiting their prospective adoptive families helped the children to begin to get to know them and their homes. However, these visits could be upsetting for some children if they meant staying away from their foster carers.

5 Moving

INTRODUCTION

After preparation for adoption, matching with and introductions to adoptive families, the children make their critical moves from foster carers or community homes into their adoptive placements. The *Supporting Adoption* study[1] notes the current practice is for these moves to be stage-managed by adoption agency staff. The study also notes that, to try to help the children through these events, they may be encouraged to take special possessions with them. At about the same time as they move homes, older children often also have to change schools. It is usually their adoptive parents who oversee this particular change in their lives.

In this chapter we report the sample children's views and experiences of their moves from being looked after by the local authority into their adoptive homes. Once again, we kept our key questions broad and explored this stage of the process by first inviting the children to tell us anything they could remember about their moves. We then asked them about the timing of the moves and who and what helped them and, in particular, whether they took any special belongings with them. We also asked if they had had to change schools when they moved and, if so, what they felt about it.

FINDINGS

Waiting to move

It was difficult for the children to quantify the time between meeting their prospective adoptive families for the first time and moving in with them. Their assessments of the length of the wait ranged from just a few days to a year-and-a-half. They were, however, able to tell us what they remembered and felt about these time periods.

---

1   See *Supporting Adoption* (Lowe and Murch, 1999) Chapter 11, Post Placement Issues.

Interestingly only Wanda (aged 12) expressed a view that they had had to wait too long to move. She said:

> To go to live with her. I think it was about six months . . . I remember being impatient and not being patient much because I couldn't wait to live with my Mum.

Wanda added that her foster family and social worker helped her to cope with the waiting by taking her out and making her feel as though they valued the time with her before she left.

Three children, however, felt they had moved too soon. One of them said she had felt happy and settled with her foster carers and had wanted to be adopted by them. She recalled that they had not told her that she would be moving 'as soon as they got the message' about her move. Consequently she felt she had not had time to think it over, let her school friends know she was leaving, and ensure that she had something to take with her to remind herself of her foster placement. Another child reflected:

> I'm not really sure . . . Looking back I think it feels like it was a bit of a short time . . . Looking back you think that was quick to get to know someone you're going to have to spend your whole life with . . . I just feel like . . . Oh wow, we did that in that short time . . .

Andy (aged 11) expressed a similar view. He felt he had not had enough time to get to know his prospective parents before he moved in with them. Implying that everyone was still on their best behaviour, he commented, 'They hadn't really shouted at us . . . ' Others had not minded waiting because the time went very quickly and explained how visits to and from their new families had helped this time to pass. When one boy (aged 12) was asked how long he had to wait before he moved, he said he thought it was about a month and,

> That was nice, because there were still introductions going through it. And then eventually we came to stay here for a week, and then we went home for another week, and then we came back, and we stayed permanently then . . .

The move

Twenty-five of the children talked to us about the day they moved from the foster or community placements to their new adoptive homes.[2] For most of them the occasion was both happy and sad, a mixture of pleasure and pain. Some recalled feeling happiness about being adopted and sadness because they were leaving other carers. Some mentioned uncomfortable journeys which contrasted with the pleasure of receiving presents and finding newly decorated bedrooms on their arrival. Others spoke of a combination of all these experiences.

Three girls, however, remembered it as a particularly upsetting day. One girl (aged 13) said:

> .I tried . . . not to cry there, so it wouldn't upset everyone else.
> But there was another time when I couldn't . . . really hold it in.
> So while [my foster brother] actually cried and having to phone
> [foster mother] and, her hearing me cry, made her cry . . .

Another recalled that she 'just didn't want to go really' and used various tactics to try to stay, including holding tightly onto the kitchen sink and repeatedly saying she wanted to go to the toilet. She said she was so upset that she cried half the way home. The third girl said:

> I was crying my eyes out and I didn't want to go. I thought the
> next day I could see [my foster carers] but I couldn't. So I really
> missed them . . .

The journeys themselves were remembered for experiences as varied as:

- it being a really 'hard drive', not having 'travelled that far before';
- travel sickness;
- not being able to see out of the car window;
- having to squeeze into the back seat of a packed car;
- a race home between the family's two cars; and
- seeing a first 'glimpse of Stonehenge'.

Justin (aged 9) described having his favourite soft toys, Panda and Rabbit, sitting next to him in the back of the car.

---

2   None of the children in the sample moved directly from their birth families to their adoptive families.

When asked if anyone was especially helpful with the move, some of the children remembered their foster carers, residential workers, social workers, and friends offering them reassurances as they left, such as:

> *Not to worry. Nothing bad's gonna happen. You'll have a nice time there and you can always still keep in contact. And you can do different things.*

Adoptive parents were also remembered as being supportive by encouraging the children not to be scared. Other children recalled being reassured and comforted physically. One of them said:

> *And it took us up 'til three o'clock to move in and then at five o'clock [our social worker] went and we sat in here and watched TV. And I sat on Mum's knee and [sister] sat on Dad's knee and then we swapped over . . . We sat on their knee for about an hour each.*

One girl, who found the experience very upsetting, spoke at some length about the support her adoptive parents gave her on that particular day. She seemed to appreciate their provision of distractions:

Girl	*When after all the social workers had gone and everything and we'd had a cup of tea or something and they sent us upstairs there were presents on the bed. And taking them downstairs and opening them . . . That really made the day go by faster because you were thinking about the things you were getting and because . . . you were having a good time and weren't able to feel, think that you know you should be happy like this, because you've just been adopted. You've just moved in with someone you've been with for so and so . . . amount of time. No one said to you, 'Look this is happening to you and you're doing this'. I think that was better really . . . We dressed up for the occasion.*
Interviewer	*And was anyone especially helpful when you moved?*
Girl	*I think Mum and Dad because they didn't expect too much of us . . . They just . . . they were nice, they just didn't say anything. 'Oh, you're not feeling too upset'*

... They didn't worry ... and keep asking you if you were all right. They just got on really, giving you the presents ... Some other people might have done that which would have made it harder because they would have kept reminding you. But Mum and Dad just didn't keep saying that, which was good. So I think they were really helpful.

Ten children spoke enthusiastically about receiving presents on that day. Some received teddies and other soft toys. Corine (aged 11) arrived at her new home to find a collection of 25 teddies in a hammock in her bedroom. One boy (aged 12) found all his new toys pleasantly overwhelming.

Boy	*Well, I can remember that it's, like, I went in and I was like, 'Oooh, a house all to myself with these people' ... So I went upstairs to my room and I was amazed to find that there was all these toys in the wardrobes and things and cupboards and barrels and things like that.*
Interviewer	*For you?*
Boy	*Yeah, and I said 'Is there another person here?' and they said, 'No, all these things are for you', and I nearly fainted ...*

The children also spoke appreciatively about the changes made to their bedrooms in preparation for their arrivals – the new beds, duvet covers, dressing tables, bean bags, lamps, books and book shelves.

Special belongings

All but two of the 25 children who were asked if they had taken something special with them when they moved, said that they had. Understandably, some of the special qualities of these particular possessions seemed to be associated with the significance of the person who had given them to the child. Their value was also explained by one boy who, when asked how it helped to bring his special things, answered:

It helped a lot because it reminded me of what happened and I'll never forget.

Over half of this sub-sample of children told us that they had moved with one or more treasured teddy bear, soft toy or doll. Five of them mentioned that their soft toys were presents from their birth parents or grandparents. Other soft toys were important because they were gifts from special foster carers. Other valued possessions included photographs, ornaments, computer games, a television, favourite videos and story books, a bean bag and clothes. More unusually, one girl said she had brought her 'special stuff' with her, which she described as sweets she had saved for about two weeks before her move. She added that when she was saving them she sometimes felt really hungry and would 'look at them without eating them'.

Lucy (aged 10), who felt she had moved to her adoptive placement too quickly, said her life story book was the only thing she had brought with her. As noted above, she said if she had had more time to prepare for her move she felt she could have 'got something to remind me' of her foster placement. Another girl had a jewellery box and some books from her foster placements but did not regard these as special. She said that prior to her adoptive placement she had moved at least 17 times and when asked if anything special had moved with her she replied:

> No, not really . . . I usually lost things. I didn't have many, very many things because I kept on moving and they were usually stuck up the attic, so I forgot them. . . So I didn't really have anything that moved.

Although some of the children's special possessions had subsequently been put up in the loft or upstairs on a shelf, others were still an important part of their daily lives. For instance, three of them said that their teddies and dolls, which they variously described as dirty, old, scruffy and torn apart, were, and sometimes still are, their confidantes. As one girl (aged 8) explained:

> She was someone I could talk to. When I was smaller I'd talk to her . . . She was my best friend when I was smaller. I still talk to her sometimes now. . . 'cause she went everywhere I went. Like she was comforting.

This girl showed her interviewer her doll which had recently been to a dolls' hospital. One of her brothers commented that the doll was still very important to his sister and suggested that she had found her recent separation from it whilst it was being repaired very hard to endure.

Other precious soft toys were always kept in bed and groomed regularly. However, one treasured possession had been lost and another damaged. Chantelle (aged 9) only had a photograph of her prized teddy and wistfully described how, on the day of her move, it must have dropped out of the car. Another girl's special bean bag had been sent to the rubbish-tip because her new adoptive brother accidentally spilt some sticky paint on it. The interviewer suspected it was an understatement when she said, with a smile, that she had 'told him off'.

Making adjustments

These moves meant significant changes in virtually every aspect of the children's lives. Summing up her whole experience of moving, Karen (aged 13) said:

> Meet new family, meet new friends, meet new cousins, meet new houses, meet new schools. Everything really. Meet a new world.

Similarly Ian (aged 12) listed some of the many changes he had had to cope with:

> You have to get used to the home, have to get used to where you live and the places outside. It's not what you're used to. Your next door neighbours. You have to get used to everything really.

It is therefore not surprising that when we asked the children our broad questions about their visits, moves and special possessions, emergent themes were the strangeness of their new relationships and environments, and the many adjustments they had had to make. Although they appreciated opportunities to begin to get to know their prospective parents and family homes prior to their moves, to keep some of their special possessions and to be welcomed with gifts and newly decorated bedrooms, it is understandable that their early days in their new placements were often still experienced as puzzling and stressful.

Just two of the children talked about the first few weeks and months in their adoptive homes exclusively in terms of the newness of everything being exciting, but they did not elaborate on their experiences.

Early difficulties in relationships with adoptive parents

Seven of the children spoke specifically about early difficulties in their relationships with their adoptive parents. One of them remembered having big arguments with her new parents and that she 'got upset about lots of things'. Consequently she would often go to her bedroom to 'cry and cry'. Another child simply recalled that she was really nasty to her mother when she first moved.

One of the girls described how she and her mother had to 'learn to put up with each other and live with each other'. She had found it hard to adjust to her adoptive mother's rules, which were different from those of her foster carers. The example of a new rule she gave was having to tidy her room if she wanted some pocket money. She also spoke of her mother having views which were different from her previous carers. She explained:

> She is a Christian. So through her I've seen, I've learned about God and Jesus and I could say I'm part Christian now, but I'm not as enthusiastic as her. She has different views about God and things.

Then the girl explained how her mother had had to learn to 'put up with' her, saying, '... like my anger. She had to learn about that ...' She concluded:

> You both have to make the effort to know each other and to feel comfortable about living with each other.

Another child had difficulties of a slightly different nature when he first moved. He remembered his adoptive mother and father used to contradict each other, so he was confused about what he should and should not be doing. He said, 'it was a bit of pain but then we sorted it out'.

Additionally, most of the children had had to get used to families which were different in size and structure, or as one child put it, 'type', to those of their birth and foster families. One girl (aged 12), who moved from a placement with just foster carers to an adoptive family with two birth children, recalled how it was odd having some other people around, ''cause there was a lot more people around here than there was there'. However, she positively described the early development of her relationship with her adoptive brother. She said he was quiet at first, but soon started 'going his normal way ...' and 'he was playing with me and showing me how to work the computer and we were just messing around easily'.

Fiona, one of the youngest children in the sample, found her new surroundings very confusing. She described how 'everything was unusual and people were rushing around a lot . . . ' She joined older siblings and recalled how, when she first moved, 'I wasn't quite sure who [they] were, because I thought they was just visitors'. It is important to note that she experienced this confusion despite having been given an introductory book which explained all the family relationships.

The experience of getting to know extended family for the first time was only described in detail by one girl. She felt nervous about meeting two young cousins for the first time. She connected her nervousness to her realisation that her joining the family would have an impact on her parents' wider family relationships. She understood that, until her arrival, the cousins had been the only children to whom her parents were close. She explained:

> I guess sometimes I felt that when I met them they wouldn't
> appreciate us being there because . . . they were used to being
> the only children in Mum and Dad's lives . . . When [my sibling]
> and I were there . . . they would get a quarter of the attention
> rather than half of the attention . . .

Environmental and cultural changes

There were other environmental and cultural changes for the children to handle. One of the girls commented that her new house smelt and felt different from her foster home. She added that she liked the smell and feel of the house and still notices them sometimes when she returns home after a few days away. One girl (aged 10) spoke of having to adjust to a new family diet. Her mother had served curry for her first tea which she did not like because it was spicy. When she told her mother she was given chips instead which she thought were OK. Since then she has learnt to like curry. Another girl described how she had gone to a birthday party for the first time with her new parents and, because of her previous experiences of birthday parties with her foster families, she had expected it to be on a beach. Expressing disappointment, she explained that the party was just a house party.

In the course of discussing all the changes they had to cope with, three of the children mentioned that, not surprisingly, it was sometime before they felt settled. When John (aged 14) first moved he did not want to go out for the first two weeks because he did not know anyone. Ian said, 'Like I've got used to it now, but it takes a while to get used to it'. His sister similarly said that it took a long time to adjust.

Changing schools

We asked 25 of the children about their experience of changing schools when they moved. Five of them welcomed the opportunity to change schools saying that their new schools were nice, really good and OK. One of the girls liked the change because it was a chance to make new friends. Another, who was of mixed heritage, was especially pleased to move to a new school. She had moved from a rural town, where she thought she was the only black person, to a racially mixed inner city area, and said,

Girl   *I was the only black person in that school.*

Interviewer   *Right. And you're not now? Is that what you're saying?*

Girl   *I'm not. I'm the millionth, millionth* [black] *person . . . That's why I felt settled in the school.*

Ruth (aged 11) saw changing schools as both a positive and negative experience. She said it was, 'very scary 'cause you don't know anyone there . . . but it was exciting as well'.

The majority of the children, however, only talked about changing schools in negative terms describing it as scary, hard and strange. The most common difficulties associated with the change were not knowing anyone, including the teachers, and having to make new friends. Some of the children missed their old friends and teachers they particularly liked. Mandy, who did not differentiate this particular change of school from others she had experienced, said:

> *I think I've been to a lot of schools. More than anybody else . . . I thought it was a nuisance 'cause you had to leave all your friends and had to make new ones, and then leave them and make new ones.*

Another girl pointed out that, 'It was hard, the fact that everyone else had been there so long and knew each other and you were different'. She had a strong desire to return to her previous school. Another explained that she felt embarrassed that she did not know anybody and so shy that she 'just wanted to stay at home'.

Three of the children did in fact have breaks from school, and all its demands, in the early days of their placements. This was presumably so they could settle into their home, before coping with an additional change. The breaks varied in length from a few days to six weeks to four or five months.

As well as having to make new friends, the children had to get to grips with unfamiliar school systems and buildings. For instance, one girl said she found her school 'weird at first . . . ' because 'I didn't really understand the system – they had Prep One and up to Six and then they had Kindergarden and Nursery'. Another said that her new school was a lot larger than her previous one and she found it quite overwhelming.

Some of the support the children received to help them through this particular change came from other children. For instance, when Ruth was asked who helped her settle into school, she mentioned two girls who were good and nice to her and have been her friends ever since. Another girl, Karen (aged 13), said all the children in her school helped her by saying, 'Hi', and telling her their names. Janine did not mention the other children in particular, but found a combination of visiting the school for a second look around, seeing the headteacher, and going to a school party helpful. She said:

A couple of people there were really nice. Well, most, they were
all nice really. So that helped a lot going to the party and having a
good time there . . .

One child's move to her new school was made more difficult for her by other children in her new neighbourhood and school. The first time Sophie (aged 12) took her new bike and balls out to play, the local children 'took the mickey out of me . . . ' for speaking with a Scottish accent. She then feared she would be picked on at school and delayed her start by a day. Her fears were well founded. She said, '. . . the first day at school everybody kept calling me "Scottish, go back to the place that you came from"...' Understandably, she did not want to return the following day. When she did, she learnt that everybody had been told off about it. She added that although she still speaks with her Scottish accent they do not take the mickey out of her anymore.

SUMMARY

The main points in this chapter are:

- The children experienced the move itself as both a happy and sad occasion – happy because they were being adopted, but sad because they were leaving other carers to whom they were attached. They valued reassurances from their adoptive parents, foster carers, social workers and friends as they left. They also appreciated the presents they received and the changes that had been made to their bedrooms in preparation for their arrival. Most of the children (92 per cent)[3] had taken one or more prized possessions with them when they moved, some of which were still important parts of their daily lives.
- A few children (12 per cent)[4] felt they had moved in with their new families too soon after meeting them and that they had not had enough time to get to know them.
- The moves meant significant changes in almost every aspect of the children's lives – a new family, home, neighbourhood, school and friends. They had to cope with new relationships and a strange environment and make many adjustments. The early days of their new placements were often experienced as puzzling and stressful, and six children remembered having difficulties in their relationships with their new parents.
- Changing schools was scary, hard and strange, particularly because the children did not know anyone, including teachers, and had to make new friends. They also had to get used to unfamiliar school systems and environments. Other children sometimes helped the adopted children to settle in.[5]

---

3   Based on a sub-sample of 25 children.
4   Based on a sub-sample of 25 children.
5   See Chapter 9, *Adoptive Home and School*, p.111.

6   **Court**

INTRODUCTION

After moving into their adoptive home, the children experience another period of waiting before a court considers an application made by their adoptive parents for an adoption order. Adoption orders legally transfer parental responsibility from children's birth parents and local authorities to adoptive parents.[1] Decisions are taken by the courts following at least one hearing. As applicants, adoptive parents must appear in court. The children do not have to attend the hearings. Guardians *ad litem*, if they are appointed, are required to make recommendations about the children's attendance.[2]

Children cannot be parties to the proceedings unless the application is heard in the High Court,[3] so they are not commonly legally represented. However, in contested cases guardians *ad litem* are involved. The guardian's role is to safeguard the children's interests, but unlike guardians in care proceedings they do not actively represent the children.

Although applications for adoption orders can technically be made in the case of agency placements when children have been in their adoptive placement for at least 13 weeks,[4] in practice adopters have to, or choose to, wait longer before making their applications. The time between the children being placed and parents lodging their applications with the court depends upon a number of factors: the original purpose of the placement; the children's legal route to adoption; possible birth parental opposition and, not least, the development of relationships between the children and their new families.

---

1   See Adoption Act 1976, ss 12 and 39. For further details, see *Supporting Adoption* (Lowe and Murch, 1999), Chapter 2, The Legal Background.
2   Adoption Rules 1984, r 18(6)(b).
3   Adoption Rules 1984, r 15(2)(k). Most applications for adoption are currently heard in the county courts.
4   Adoption Act, 1976, s 13. But in the case of foster carers subsequently adopting the period is 12 months.

Within our sample, adoption was the original purpose of the placement for the majority of children.[5] It includes, however, some children who were placed initially with long-term foster carers who subsequently decided to apply for adoption and also three children whose short-term foster placements evolved into long-term foster placements before becoming adoptive ones.

The children's legal pathways to adoption will also have varied. The route may have been a straightforward one, and not been preceded by freeing proceedings.[6] It may, however, have involved an application for freeing for adoption by the local authority. The outcome of such proceedings will usually have been known before the children were placed in their adoptive homes. However, some children may have been placed for adoption during the course of freeing proceedings, and the prospective adopters and the children may have had to wait for these other legal tangles to unravel before an application for an adoption order could have been made.

The children's adoptive parents may also have chosen to delay making an application because it may have taken the children more than three months to settle into their new families enough to be ready to make this legal attachment. Parents may need more time themselves before they feel sure enough of the placement to apply to make it legally binding. Given the irreversible nature of adoption, time may be needed for settling in and unhurried decisions to be made.

The *Supporting Adoption* study[7] indicates that, once an application for an adoption order has been made, the legal procedures and processes of adoption may take a remarkably long time. As earlier research undertaken by the team has shown, it may take a matter of years rather than weeks or months (Murch *et al*, 1993). The development of the placement will have been assessed. The court may have appointed a guardian *ad litem*, a Reporting Officer, or both, to interview the birth parents. The progress of the proceedings may also have been affected by the children's birth parents exercising their right to contest the applications actively in court or simply by

---

5   See Chapter 2, *Methodology*.
6   *Supporting Adoption* (Lowe and Murch, 1999) notes that a "freeing order" is an order (which can only be granted upon an agency application) which has the effect of ending the birth parents' interest in the child so that they can no longer object to the adoption. See Chapter 13, The Legal Process, p.247.
7   See *Supporting Adoption* (Lowe and Murch, 1999), Chapter 13.

withholding their agreement.[8] Additionally, as Murch *et al* point out, '. . . there is sometimes a substantial element of avoidable delay' (Murch *et al*, 1993).

In this chapter we report our sample children's views of this complex and unpredictable stage of the process. We first asked them about their experience of the waiting period between moving and the order being made.[9] We then established if they had attended the final hearing themselves. If they had not, we explored what they knew about the court hearing and whether they had wanted to attend. If they did go, we first invited them to tell us anything about it. If appropriate, we then asked questions about their preparation, experience with the judiciary, and whether they found attending the final hearing to be a helpful experience.

FINDINGS

Fear of going to court[10]

When the children were asked whether they had been to court, it emerged that the prospect of having to go was worrying for some of the children. Overall, 20 children, including children of all ages and both boys and girls, expressed fears and worries about having to attend the court.

Nine-year-old Justin described the nature of these fears and his personal coping strategy. While Justin was recounting this experience his fear was almost palpable. Earlier in the interview he had been talking gleefully about burying jelly fish alive while on holiday. When he moved on to describe his court experience, he spoke in a whisper and his voice

---

8 We do not know how many of the children in our sample had contested adoption proceedings. We used questionnaires completed by adoptive parents for the *Supporting Adoption* study to gather information about the children's backgrounds. The questionnaire had not asked parents whether the adoption proceedings were contested. Figures quoted by Ryburn suggest that, by 1984, 11 per cent of final adoption hearings were contested and that the figures have risen ever since to 30 per cent of non-parent adoption orders in 1995 (Ryburn, 1998).

9 After consideration, we did not think it reasonable to expect the children to try to distinguish between the waiting period from moving to the application being made and the waiting time from the application to the final hearing.

10 For the prospective adopters' experience of going to court, see *Supporting Adoption* (Lowe and Murch, 1999) Chapter 13, The Legal Process, para 2.3.

changed to that of a much younger child.

Justin	*Well, I was very scared the night before so I hid a sword in my duvet – 'cause I was scared. I didn't get told off though because my Mum said it was OK.*
Interviewer	*You hid a sword?*
Justin	*Yeah, but not a real one, it was a pretend.*
Interviewer	*What was the sword for?*
Justin	*Because I was very, very scared.*
Interviewer	*Do you remember what you were scared about?*
Justin	*Yeah, the judge himself . . .*
Interviewer	*The judge himself. What did you think he was going to do?*
Justin	*I thought . . . he was going to be all mean and hammer the hammer down . . . that sort of wooden thing . . . that they . . . when they go 'Order in the courts' . . .*
Interviewer	*Can you tell me anything more about the sword – what the sword was for?*
Justin	*I was scared because I had never seen a judge before – that's the first time I ever did and I never knew what it was going to be like. So I was scared.*

A few other children shared Justin's feelings and described the idea of having to go to court as scary. Others remembered being nervous or worried. Some children similarly explained their fears in terms of not knowing what the court or judge would be like. A few expected a criminal court: they imagined there would be a jury and many other people present, including the police and MPs, and that they would have to swear an oath.

There was a clear and understandable association for the children between having to go to court and wrong-doing. This was illustrated by an eight-year-old girl when she was asked whether she had been to court. Sounding quite indignant, she said she had not been. Her slightly older sister, who was being interviewed with her, interrupted and told her that she had in fact been to court. For a moment the younger girl was adamant that she had not, adding, 'I wasn't bad'. After a slight pause, the interviewer began to explain why she might have been to court and the girl interrupted with 'Oh yes I did,' adding a few moments later, '. . . not like going to court for being naughty'. The child then began to remember something about the experience.

Two other girls were also worried that the order would not be granted. One said:

> I was worried whether I would be allowed to get adopted or not.
> And if I was not, what would I do and where would I go?
> [Laughing nervously]

The other explained that she thought the judge was going to say 'No'. When she was asked why she thought that, she just said matter-of-factly, 'Because some judges do'.

Individual children expressed different fears. One child recalled that he was very unsure about his own role: what he would have to say and do. He also remembered wondering how long the hearing would last. Another, who was not in contact with her birth parents, was frightened that she might see them at court.

By contrast, three children responded to questions about going to court with unreservedly positive feedback about the idea of having to go. Two of them remembered being excited by the prospect. Another was pleased to have an excuse for an extra day off school.

There was some evidence that apprehension about having to go to court interfered with earlier stages of the adoption process. One boy (aged 14) described his reaction when his social worker and key-worker asked him about the kind of adoptive family he wanted. He climbed a tree and said 'I'm not gonna tell you'. A little later he explained:

> But they asked me about the family, if I wanted just Mum, a Dad,
> or both. I felt I didn't want to go to court as I was scared about it.
> That's why I didn't want to tell them.

Another child described how he felt when his foster carers asked him whether he wanted to be adopted by them. He said he did not really care 'if he did or didn't' and that he just 'wasn't sure about it'. When he was asked what he was not sure about he replied that it was having to go to the court because he thought when you go to the court you have to go there because you have done something wrong.

Preparation for court

We asked questions about the children's preparation for court and 11 children told us something about it. They remembered their parents and social workers saying that:

- there was 'nothing to worry about';
- they would be in a small room with just a judge and their family and friends;
- there wouldn't be a jury; and
- that it would be calm.

Such reassurances and explanations, and possibly others which did not emerge during the interviews, did not seem to allay the children's pre-court fears. The children remembered still feeling nervous on the day and were often surprised by the environment and nature of the proceedings. As Mike (aged 9) explained:

> Yeah, my Mum and Dad were helping me quite a lot and saying it's all right to go to court. And I just didn't believe them because I thought I'd done something wrong and they were just trying to kid me.

The waiting period between moving to the adoptive family home and the court hearing

It was difficult to get an accurate picture from the children of the lengths of time they carried these fears.[11] We asked 28 of the sample whether they remembered how long, once they had moved, they had to wait to go to court. It was followed up with exploratory questions about whether they had waited a long or short time. Four children could not remember anything about it. Another four, including three from the same family, thought it was

---

11 See Chapter 2, *Methodology*.

just a short period of time. Ian (aged 12) said:

> *Not very long. It was about four months or a few weeks. It wasn't*
> *very long until we had to get adopted and go to the court and*
> *say we'd like to be adopted. It didn't take very long.*

Six children remembered waiting significant lengths of time, but in retrospect seemed to find this acceptable. Peter (aged 11), who expressed no particular fear of going to court, for instance, said the following:

Peter | *And it happened another three years later – or two years later.*

Interviewer | *What was it like to wait two or three years?*

Peter | *I just waited.*

Interviewer | *You just waited?*

Peter | *I got a bit excited when it came to that month.*

Interviewer | *Did anyone help you with the waiting?*

Peter | *No. I just went on normal until it happened.*

The other half of this sub-sample, however, felt they had to wait too long. Corine (aged 11) described waiting as 'not nice', and explained that she just wanted to '... go and get it over and done with'.

In addition to having to manage the fear of going to court, some of the children remembered other difficulties. Three of the girls spoke of their awareness of their parents' correspondence or telephone calls with courts and local authorities. Mary (aged 9) recalled that it took ages for a form that her parents sent to the court to be returned and wished it had not taken so long. Also referring to court papers, Anna (aged 14) remembered that she had to 'wait around for the post and everything, waiting for it all to come through'. (She also mentioned finding it frustrating that when the papers eventually arrived, she was not allowed to read them. She explained, 'I wanted to know exactly what they said about us all, about whether it was going to be alright and everything, but never mind'.) Similarly, eight-year-old Helen described how 'every time the 'phone rung I thought it was the Council to say I can be adopted'.

One girl (aged 13) found the continuation of social worker's visits during this period particularly difficult. She saw the purpose of the visits as 'to check how you're doing,' and that, 'If you don't show them that you're doing well, something will happen'. Describing the positive aspects of going to court, she said:

> So getting rid of all the social workers was really good. Spending a whole year with social workers monitoring you every so often didn't really feel like it was a normal home. You know, felt like it was different to everyone else because no one else had social workers knocking at their door.

Two other children also experienced delays and were the only ones to mention reasons for them. A boy said:

> We were meant to have it in July and it wasn't. It was a year after. They set a date for July the first and it wasn't July the first that year. It was the next year . . .

He understood that his proceedings were held up because his birth mother was not 'signing the form'. One of the girls also understood that her birth mother withheld her agreement. She directed her anger about the delay towards herself and explained:

Girl   *Mum came home and she just burst into tears because my birth mum hadn't signed the papers . . . for me to be adopted to her. And she eventually signed the papers, but at that time she refused to sign the papers for me to be adopted. So she was really upset about that.*

Interviewer   *And what did you feel about that?*

Girl   *I started to cry too because I was really looking forward to being adopted and I knew things would be better for me and for my mum. So I was quite disappointed and angry, not necessarily at my birth mum, but I think mainly at me . . .*

Interviewer   *You were angry at yourself?*

Girl   *Yeah. But I didn't know why, but I remember being angry.*

Both children had a similar understanding of their birth mothers' reticence. The girl felt sympathy for her birth mother's experience of loss and explained:

> I don't know really why, but I think even now it was because my
> sister had gone to live with somebody else then and she'd lost
> both of us . . .

Some of these children explained what helped them through these waiting periods. For example, nine-year-old Thomas's adoptive mother encouraged him to think of his adoption as a journey. He explained:

> Mum referred to it as like a train. And then we started, and then
> we were going along, and we had to stop at a station, and we go
> along again, and we break down, and then we got stuck up a
> hill. Stuff like that . . .

David (aged 12) who remembered having to wait about a year for his court hearing suggested that 'just getting to know each other' helped him through this period.

The court hearing

With two exceptions, the children were able to tell us something about their experience of actually going to court and the hearing itself. For some of the children who expressed fears, the reality of the experience was not as frightening as the thought of it. As one child said, 'It wasn't as bad as I thought it was going to be'.

A few remembered long journeys and commented on the buildings themselves. Courts were described as big and compared with hospitals and airports with many doors and corridors and large waiting areas. Some children recalled having to wait a long time in corridors and hallways which contrasted with 'only' or 'just' five, ten, twenty or thirty minutes with the judge.

Although we can assume from their descriptions that most children were seen by Judges in Chambers, a minority may have had their hearings in court rooms, in what they described as massive rooms. This was particularly distressing for Sophie (aged 12) who was seen by the judge alone with her social worker. She said she found it difficult to pay attention to what was happening. She looked around everywhere and thought the room was very big. She felt scared and shaky because when the judge was talking his voice echoed around the whole room. She wanted to run to her mother and father who she could see behind glass. She said the judge talked very loudly, but thought that was the way judges had to talk. She said he made her feel really upset and that she cried.

Many of the children commented on the judge's appearance. Two of the older children said that their judges did not look like judges because they were wearing normal suits and one of them was expressly disappointed that her judge was not wearing a wig. Others remembered seeing judges who were dressed in wigs and robes, or as one of the children put it, a 'funny suit' and 'white wig thing'. Six of the children mentioned being offered a wig to try on. This was enjoyable for most, but not all of them. One of the children was clearly frightened by these clothes. Fiona (aged 9), who said she had been to court just a few months before she was interviewed, described how she covered her eyes and did not look at the judge's face because he looked wicked, wearing 'fake hairs' and 'one of those black things around him'. She saw another person wearing what she called 'them black things', who she thought was another judge, and felt so scared she hid behind her mother.

The majority of the children, however, had positive memories of their interactions with the judiciary. Judges, referred to by one child as 'the law men' were variously described as friendly, smiling, nice and funny. Peter commented:

> He wasn't like a boring old judge who's always going, 'Sit up straight' an' all that. He was pretty funny.

Two of the young girls were very pleased with the teddy bears their judges gave them. Other children were given cards.

Talking to the judge

Of the 18 children who recollected being spoken to by the judge, most recalled being asked about their wishes and feelings about being adopted. They remembered being asked questions like:

- 'Do you want to be adopted?'
- 'What's it like living with this mum?' followed by, 'Do you want the adoption to go ahead?'

- 'Are you worried about spending the rest of your lives with your Mum and Dad?', 'Are you happy to do that?', and 'Is everything OK?'

Kirsty recalled that she had nearly said 'No' because, in her words, she did not know whether to say 'No' or 'Yes'.

Some children expressed pleasure at also being asked about their nicknames, hobbies and being told jokes. Three children also remembered the judge announcing at some time during the proceedings that they were adopted.

By contrast, Steve (aged 14) viewed the hearing as an anti-climax after a long wait. He explained:

> It's just in there, saying that you actually want to live with these parents, and that's it. It's as easy as that. It's a long time for the adoption day to actually come up, but when we came to it, just a quick twenty minutes that was it! Two years for this twenty minutes.

Another child expressed disappointment with the hearing because her adoptive father's solicitor did all the talking and she and her sister were not given an opportunity to talk to the judge themselves.

Was it helpful to go to court?

Fifteen of the sample talked about the value of the experience of going to court. Most of them said they found it helpful to go because of the outcome of the proceedings. They saw it as a means to an end. By going to court they got a 'nice new family' or a family that would help and look after them.

Riahanna was pleased she went because she received information which confirmed that she will be able to see her birth mother when she is older. Another girl said:

> It was helpful 'cause that's when you really know when you are adopted. Instead of saying 'Am I adopted yet? Am I adopted yet?' you know. You can go to one place, they can say, 'You're adopted,' and you go back and then you know you're adopted.

Simon explained:

> Well, it made me feel better because I know I was actually gonna stick there forever.

A girl (aged 13) expressed a similar view:

> I think someone said that we didn't have to go to court for the actual adoption, but I'm not sure. I don't know if that was another court thing. I wanted to go to court actually to watch everything being finalised . . . seeing like the case being closed . . . the book shut on it really . . . I love reading the ending of a book because of the feeling of triumph that you've finished it . . . and I guess that was the same feeling in court, watching them close the book, really shutting it . . . Knowing that nothing else was going to happen. It was just going to be an ordinary life from now on . . .

John, expressing more ambivalence, commented:

> It didn't really mean much to me. I didn't really need the adoption day because I'd been living here, hadn't I, for just under two years . . . I was here to stay, I knew that . . . I was staying here full stop.

Nevertheless, he also felt that it had been important for him to be there to express his wish to stay where he was. He felt the court needed him and his parents to be present before a decision could be made.

Celebrations

Adoption Day celebrations

Thirty-two of the overall sample were asked about Adoption Day celebrations. After the court hearings, all but two families in this sub-sample celebrated. Just two of the girls said that afterwards they went straight back to school.

The celebrations usually included special meals at the children's favourite cafés, burger bars or pizza houses. Families also had parties, including Adoption Day cakes, family outings, presents, and took photographs. It was common for the children to celebrate in more than one way. The children celebrated in several ways. As Mark (aged 11) recalled:

> We went out then, had a few pictures and my Mother and Father
> were buying stuff for me around [town]. Practically whatever I
> wanted! And then we went and got [my cousins] from school
> and went out for a meal . . .

Anna described her various celebrations:

> I had me ears [pierced] – we were talking about it anyway. I really
> wanted my ears pierced and we went to a café and I had tons of
> cakes. I got to pick the cake I really wanted. [Laughing] But we
> really enjoyed ourselves though. And then when we got home
> we had a major dip meal and with chicken nuggets and all sorts.

Many other children remembered exactly what they had eaten and drunk. Ruth (aged 11) said, 'special chocolate – it's like hot chocolate with cream on the top and a flake – I had that'. Judy (aged 11) recalled:

> And afterwards we went to the pizza place and we had this, like,
> . . . massive milk shake. It was about that big! . . . 'Cause it was a
> really special occasion . . . And we weren't really allowed to buy
> sweets, but Daddy gave us some money so we could turn this
> thing to get some jelly beans out. I love jelly beans.

Paul (aged 12) remembered having champagne. Dione (aged 15) said her family had had a 'massive bottle of Le Piat D'Or that we'd saved to celebrate when I'd got adopted'.

There were more unusual elements to some celebrations. Wanda said she opened a bank account. Thomas very excitedly recounted that he had a surprise trip on an aeroplane. Ellie (aged 10) said that at her family party there was a large piece of silk with 'Ellie [and her siblings] are living with us' printed on it. Finally John had a special outfit, 'I had like shoes like this, slippers, shiny black shoes, pair of green, dark green trousers, white polo neck and a silk waistcoat'.

Adoption Day anniversaries

Twenty-six of the sample were asked whether they do anything special when that day comes around every year. Forty-per-cent of this sub-sample celebrated, or at least acknowledged, the anniversary in some way. Most of the children and their families have a special meal. Wanda explained:

> We usually go out places, like for a meal . . . we don't have
> anything major like a big party and things like that, but just go for
> a meal, picnic and it's fun. I think it's important that you spend
> time with each other . . .

Andy (aged 11) and Fiona (aged 9) receive presents, and Anna has a special meal and receives cards.

Six children who do not currently celebrate their Adoption Day, expressed a wish to do so. Two siblings explained:

Boy	*Well, funny you should mention this. [My sister's] social worker . . . came round when, after [my sister] had been adopted and I actually found out that day was my actual anniversary of my Adoption Day . . . It was only when I was showing [my sister's social worker] my book that we realised it was . . . And we didn't really do anything really. I asked Mum whether we should celebrate and she said, 'Well we never really do, do we?' . . .*
Interviewer	*Would you like to celebrate it?*
Boy & girl	*Yes.*
Interviewer	*You would?*
Boy	*Only for the food.*
Girl	*And the presents.*

Thomas also said:

> Last year we forgot. This year we forgot. We forget the days that
> it comes on. Mum said that I think this year we're going to
> celebrate it, because this year we're going to remember.

There were, however, about as many children who did not celebrate the anniversary or who, like Mandy, could not 'even remember when it was', who did not express any desire to mark it.

In response to questions about Adoption Day anniversaries, two of the girls mentioned anniversaries of their moves. Three other children talked about annual parties organised by their adoption agencies for, as Mark put it, '... all the people that got adopted in the neighbourhood ...' These were enjoyed for the food and discos, but more particularly for the opportunities to stay up really late.

SUMMARY

The main points raised by the children about their court experiences are:

- The prospect of having to go to court was frightening for half (48 per cent) the children. Underlying their fears were:
  - fantasies of formidable judges;
  - associations between having to go to court and wrong-doing;
  - the possibility that the order would not be granted and uncertainties about what would then happen;
  - uncertainties about the nature of the proceedings;
  - uncertainties about their own role in proceedings; and
  - possibilities of unwanted meetings with birth parents.
- Apprehension about having to go to court interfered with some children's feelings about earlier stages of the adoption process.
- Social workers' and adoptive parents' verbal reassurances and explanations about having to go to court did not always effectively allay the children's pre-court fears.
- Although a fifth of a sub-sample of 28 children found it acceptable to wait a long time to go to court, half felt they had had to wait too long. The court hearing was sometimes experienced as an anti-climax after a long wait.
- Two-thirds (66 per cent)[11] of a sub-sample of children particularly valued the experience of attending the court hearing because of the positive outcome of the proceedings. The majority of children (90 per cent)[12] had positive memories of their interactions with the judiciary. Although courts seemed large and imposing buildings, the reality of going to court was rarely as frightening as the thought of having to go.
- The majority of children (94 per cent)[13] celebrated their Adoption Day and ten of them celebrated its anniversary.

---

11 Based on a sub-sample of 15 children.
12 Based on a sub-sample of 38 children.
13 Based on a sub-sample of 32 children.

7 Life Story Work

INTRODUCTION

Life story work, as we have already noted, can have several aims. Fahlberg (1994) suggests that it provides a chronology of children's lives and helps them to understand and remember what has happened in the past. Life story work can also be used to enhance self-esteem and identity. Additionally it can be used as a therapeutic tool to help a child resolve strong emotions about past events, especially those relating to experiences of separation and loss. As Ryan and Walker (1993) point out, the work may result in a book or video, or simply a record of sessions which took place. They argue:

> It does not have to result in a product – it is the process rather
> than just the product which will yield most benefits for the
> children and young people involved.

With regard to its timing, they point out that it is sometimes done as part of a child's preparation to move to a new family, but can otherwise be undertaken at another time to '. . . help the child accept life as it is' (Ryan and Walker, 1993). It may be started as a discrete piece of work, but it can be added to later.

The findings about life story work reported here supplement those recorded in Chapter 3, which specifically concerned the life story work the children associated with being introduced to the idea of adoption. The findings in this chapter more broadly concern any of the children's past, present or future life story work.

We began to explore this topic by asking them if anyone had ever made or was planning to make a life story with them. If so, we then asked with whom it had been or would be undertaken and questioned them about the nature of the work and the resulting books. (None of the children within the sample had life story videos or memory boxes.) With our focus on support issues, we then asked whether the children found, or anticipated finding, this work helpful, and, if so, in what ways.

FINDINGS

Contents of life story books

Eighteen children showed the interviewers their life story books during the course of the interview. Although we did not ask to see them before or during the interview, 11 had them ready for us on our arrival and another seven went to fetch them during the interview when the issue was raised or at the very end of the interview.

It was not possible within the time constraints of the interviews to survey systematically the contents of the books, but our fieldwork notes show that, although the contents varied, they most commonly contained labelled photographs of:

- birth family;
- foster families;
- other carers;
- friends;
- pets; and
- holidays, birthday parties, Christmases and other special occasions.

Collectively they also contained:

- school photos and reports;
- family trees;
- maps of the children's moves when they were with their birth families and the children's own moves since leaving them;
- maternity hospital tags, a note of their birth weights, and copies of birth certificates;
- copies of court orders – care, freeing and adoption orders;
- details of the children's likes and dislikes;
- letters and cards;
- children's drawings and paintings; and
- certificates.

Some of the children had life story books that were well-bound photograph albums. Others had lever-arch files with pages protected by plastic sleeves or photograph albums with pages covered with protective peel-back cellophane. A few children had scrap books which were inadequate to cope with their heavy usage. Some had already been re-covered and others looked battered and in need of repair.

Making a life story book

Thirty-three of the 41 children had life story books and 25 of them remembered who had helped to make them, usually before they were placed for adoption. Nineteen recalled being helped by social workers, two by foster carers, and one by both. Another three children are currently being helped or will be helped in future by their adoptive parents. Dione (aged 15) was helped to make a life story book by her social worker and said it took 'Oh, weeks and weeks'. Janine (aged 13) remembered:

> We had a folder from the social worker before we moved here. I don't think it was especially to move in here . . . we had a morning, some mornings off school and did that with the social worker . . . She'd already written it and we were just reading it through and sticking in the photographs.

One girl (aged 14) made hers with her foster mother and remembered having 'major conversations over it all' as they worked. Ten-year-old Debbie's adoptive parents worked on her life story book soon after she and her siblings moved in. They received photographs of their birth parents from the social services and one of the social workers 'typed up the whole of my life story on the computer'.

At the time of the interview, Mike (aged 9) and Ellie (aged 10) were still making their life story books with their adoptive mother. Mike explained the ongoing process:

> My mum takes pictures on the beach and things and it's from when I was first born, when I was only two-and-a-quarter pounds . . . until now. When I get older [my mum will] keep on doing that life story book. My sister's started her third one.

His sister Ellie explained:

> We just get photos and put them in and write about them, like, what I was doing on that picture. Like I was opening a present or something.

Eight of the children who began their life story work with social workers mentioned that they continue to add information to the books themselves, usually photographs and certificates.

The process remained incomplete for Corine (aged 11). She remembered doing some life story work with a woman she thought was her adoptive mother's social worker. This had included work on a family tree which had not been finished before the social worker left her job and took the family tree with her.

Having a life story book

Who keeps the life story book?

The majority of children with life story books kept them in their bedrooms, playrooms or other places where they were easily accessible. However, two teenage boys, John and Steve, had their books looked after by their adoptive parents. Eleven-year-old Ruth and 13-year-old Karen also had their books looked after by their adoptive parents. Another child was not sure where hers was kept. One boy explained how he and his brother had forgotten about them and not seen them since they had been in placement, until his adoptive parents discussed the possibility of their participation in the project. He said:

> Dad gave us the cassette and leaflets and things and we were just talking about it. [Our siblings] had had this book . . . and we asked whether we had one. Mum said, 'Yes', but we haven't looked at it before. She hasn't really wanted to show us, but she got it and we had a look in it . . .

At first Sophie (aged 12) seemed a little unsure whether she had a life story book. Then she remembered drawing pictures and writing with her social worker and that there was a book that her social worker might have kept or that had been put up in the loft.

Understanding the information

Anna spoke of the importance of the use of understandable materials in life story work. She worked on a family tree with one of her social workers and when she was asked if she found it helpful, she said:

Anna   In a way. But I didn't really understand it that well then 'cause I was still quite young.

Interviewer   *How old were you . . . ?*

Anna   *About seven. And I didn't understand a thing about it*
then, because I didn't go to school. I didn't go to school
when I was with my real mum.

Ian (aged 12) mentioned that when he had looked through his life story book recently, with his adoptive mother, he had gained new insights into his birth family. He learnt from his book, apparently for the first time, that in addition to the birth siblings he lives with, he has about six half-siblings,

> *And Mum said, 'You've got three sisters and three brothers'. And*
> *I said, 'What?' . . . It's stupid. I didn't know. They should have*
> *told me . . . We've got lots of half brothers and sisters really.*

He said he had looked through the book many times before, although it was unclear whether he usually did so alone or with his adoptive parents. Ian explained his not absorbing this information in the past in terms of his learning difficulties. He also said it was the first time he could 'put up with it', perhaps suggesting that he found this information difficult to manage emotionally. He said again, angrily, that he thought it was 'just stupid' to have so many brothers and sisters. The interviewer also noticed the book contained some other information that he may not have retained. There was a copy of an advertisement of Ian and his siblings which had been placed in *Be My Parent*.[1] During the interview he said that they had not been advertised. He may not have remembered being advertised or seeing a copy of the advertisement in his book. Alternatively he may not have wanted to talk about it.

When Helen (aged 8) was first asked if she had a life story book she said she did not. At this point her adoptive mother, who was in the adjoining room with the door open, came into the room where the interview was taking place and said that Helen did in fact have one. She added:

> *I read it to her from time to time. She gets obsessed by it and we*
> *read it quite frequently and then all of a sudden it stays in the*
> *cupboard for a while.*

---

1   BAAF's Be My Parent family-finding service publishes *Be My Parent*, a bi-monthly newspaper featuring children of all ages and backgrounds needing new permanent families across the UK.

Helen seemed a little irritated by her mother's intervention and contradicted her by saying that she hardly ever read it, and then added, '. . . I only ever read it once'. The interviewer felt that she should respect Helen's original answer to the question and not pursue this further, and that, metaphorically, the topic should be put back in the cupboard.

Although, as we have said, we did not study the life story book materials systematically, our impression was that most of them contained information which was appropriate to children's understanding at the time of the interview. Others included information which appeared to be way beyond their comprehension. Nine-year-old Luke's, for instance, contained much hand-written text explaining his past which was clearly beyond his reading ability. However, there were also entries which were well within his understanding and he was particularly familiar with three of them.[2] First, he selected a picture of a garden with some text that encouraged him to think of his adoption as a transplantation. He quoted the following passage:

> *This is how I feel. Growing in the born-to family garden; pulled up from the family garden; brought into care. Plants need food from the earth to grow. Child needs love from a family to grow. Roots must be planted again.*

He turned a few more pages to a picture of a block of ice with text that suggested that he may have experienced a feeling of numbness when he left his birth family:

> *I felt sad when I left my family. The feeling was like having a solid block of ice inside me . . . When all the ice has melted I will be ready for a new family.*

Finally he found an illustration of a "love ladder" with each step reflecting a stage in the development of the child's relationship with his new parents. Luke read:

> *Honeymoon, everyone is nice to each other. Withdrawal, I'm not sure about it. Rejection, I don't like it. Adjustment, getting used to it. Ending, enjoying things together. Love, this is where it starts. Loving, loving, loving. I belong to a family. Ladder of love.*

---

2 These entries were taken from *I Want to Make a Life Story* (Burch, 1992).

The children's evaluation of life story books

Twenty-three of the 33 children who had life story books were positive about them in so far as they either said they found them helpful or they showed them to the interviewers with obvious enthusiasm and pride. Five other children expressed some conflicting feelings about them. We remained unsure about the feelings of the other five children, including Helen.

Most of those who found their life story books helpful appreciated them for reminding them about their birth families and what had happened in their pasts. For instance, Debbie (aged 10) said she found it helpful to have a life story book, 'because when I want to find out about my family, I can just look in there'. Similarly, Mandy (aged 11) said:

> I think it was a good idea, 'cause I won't forget that I was adopted – forget everything and everybody. So I thought it was a good idea.

Phil (aged 9) said he found his life story book helpful because he can 'look back'. When asked what was helpful about looking back, he explained:

> 'Cause I hardly see my Daddy Geoff. I have a few pictures of him so I can look back and remember what he looks like. And [my birth mum], I can remember what she looks like . . .

Ellie, who is still in the process of making hers, said she finds it helpful:

Ellie   *Just looking back at things like, my old Mum and everything, when I was small and things.*

Interviewer   *And how does it help you to look back?*

Ellie   *Just lets me remember and not forget.*

Wanda (aged 12) explained why she valued her book:

> I don't really understand much about my parents until I read that book and I've found it helpful to understand about them and what they like to do and . . . how they lived and everything.

Janine used hers when she was feeling unsure about things that had happened and particularly when she could not talk to anyone about something that was bothering her. She said:

> It's a bit like reading an encyclopaedia of my life . . . I can look
> through and say, 'Well, this happened at that time'.

Paul (aged 12) had a photograph album and it had 'got a bit of story life in it'. He said it was helpful to look at it sometimes because, 'other than that I wouldn't know much about my life'. He expressed a strong desire to know about his past. Paul said he would like to go back in time to see what his parents were like and,

> I'd want to see what happened to me when I was a child, when
> . . . well, I am a child still, but when I was younger.

He added, that 'if I try really hard, I'll be able to see them again'. It was not clear whether he was trying to will a real meeting or simply to picture them in his imagination.

Three children also valued their life story books because they could inform other people, as well as themselves, about their pasts. David (aged 12) said it 'helped a lot' for his social worker to write everything down and explain it to him. He also appreciated it because 'our Mum and Dad could see what happened to us'. One of the girls also said that she wanted her adoptive mother to see her life story book, particularly during their introductory period.

Five children mentioned that, although they found their books helpful, they were sometimes upset when they looked at them or else they expressed ambivalence towards them. Nicky (aged 11) said that looking at her book used to make her cry.

Nicky	It used to make me cry actually, when I first came here, but it doesn't anymore. I did not cry last night.
Interviewer	Why did it make you cry, do you think?
Nicky	Thinking about the past really.
Interviewer	What was it about the past that made you cry?
Nicky	All of it really.

Jackie (aged 8) also mentioned that sometimes she starts crying when she reads letters and cards from her birth mother. She sounded as though she was holding back tears as she showed them to the interviewer.

Two of the teenagers expressed ambivalence towards life story work. When one of them was asked whether he was glad that he had been shown his life story book after not seeing it for sometime, he said:

> I'm not really glad or not glad. It's nice to have actually seen it, but I wouldn't have been really bothered if I'd seen it or not . . . When I was looking at this thing, I didn't get kind of emotional like that, it was just normal looking at a book. Like, 'There's me when I was younger'.

He added that the only pictures in the book that he was really interested in were those of his foster carers and his birth siblings. He said he was not interested in those of his birth parents.

One of the girls and her adoptive mother have borrowed a book about making a life story book, but the girl seemed unsure about starting it. She said:

Girl   I don't mind, because it might help me in a way, but it might not help me in another way.

Interviewer First of all, how might it help you?

Girl   Well, it might help me . . . with the past and trying to forget it. But then it could bring it back and then it could just stick in my memory. So it's good and bad.

SUMMARY

The main points are:

- Over three-quarters (80 per cent) of the sample had done life story work resulting in life story books.[3] Most of the work had been undertaken by social workers prior to the children being placed for adoption. At the time of the interview eight children were continuing to add information to their books.
- The contents of the life story books varied, but their main component appeared to be labelled photographs. Most of the

---

3   In *Supporting Adoption* (Lowe and Murch, 1999), 73 per cent of the sample children had a life story record. See p.113.

books were robust enough to withstand the possibility of the children looking at them repeatedly, but some scrap books were simply inadequate for this purpose. They were usually kept by the children in easily accessible places.

- Some children mentioned or demonstrated that they did not understand or retain all the information conveyed to them during life story work or contained in their life story books.
- Seventy per cent[4] of the children who had life story books felt positive about them. Most that found them helpful did so because they informed and reminded them about their birth families and what had happened in their pasts. Five children mentioned that they were sometimes upset when they looked at them.

---

4 Based on the sub-sample of 33 children who had life story books.

8 Contact

INTRODUCTION

Since the beginning of the 1990s, there has been a significant change in practice towards more post-adoption contact (Ryburn, 1998). Although it is difficult to establish the full extent of this at a national level, the *Supporting Adoption* study (Lowe and Murch, 1999) included questions about post-adoption contact in its national postal survey of a sample of 226 families who had had children placed with them between 1992 and 1994. The responses showed that 83 per cent of the families had some kind of contact with one or more birth relatives of their adopted children. Almost half (49 per cent) of a sub-sample of 217 families had some contact with their children's birth mothers.[1]

This change in practice can be seen as part of a gradual movement away from the "clean break" approach to adoption towards adoptions characterised by less secrecy, particularly for adoptions of older children (Lowe, 1997). Underlying this movement towards greater openness was research evidence that some adopted people have a need for information about their birth families and may want to search for them (Triseliotis, 1973). There were also studies which showed that birth parents do not forget their children after they have been adopted and may continue to suffer the pain of separation from and loss of their children for a lifetime (Mullender, 1991; Bouchier, Lambert and Triseliotis, 1991; Hughes and Logan, 1993; Howe, Sawbridge, Hinings, 1997). There was also evidence from general studies of permanent placements about contact as a protective factor in permanent family placements, and its importance for children's well-being and sense of identity (Department of Health, 1991). The trend was also supported by adoption and consumer advocacy groups (Ryburn, 1998).

An important legal milestone in this movement was the Children Act 1975 which included a provision to allow adopted children access to their

---

1   See *Supporting Adoption* (Lowe and Murch, 1999), Chapter 15, Contact, p.279.

birth records.[2] The Children Act 1989 was also significant in that it imposed a new duty on local authorities to promote contact between children who were being looked after and their parents, anyone with parental responsibility for them, and any relatives or friends of the children, as long as this is consistent with the children's welfare.[3] The potential of the Act to promote contact in permanent placements is illustrated by the Guidance (Department of Health, 1991):

> *Contact, however occasional, may continue to have a value for the child even when there is no question of returning to his family. These contacts can keep alive for a child a sense of his origins and may keep open options for family relationships in later life.*

The practice of maintaining contact between adopted children and their birth families and other people from their pasts does, however, have its critics. It has been one of the main issues which has dominated discussions about adoption policy and practice since the mid-1980s (Fratter, 1996). There have been arguments about the rights of the children and their birth families to have contact with one another and questioning of the beneficial psychosocial effects of having contact (Quinton *et al*, 1997). There is currently a debate about the extent to which this practice is in fact based on sound empirical research (Ryburn, 1998; Fratter, 1996). As Triseliotis (1997) explains:

> *The arguments for and against contact have been rehearsed many times over, usually ending in a plea for more evidence.*

This chapter documents the children's views and experiences of the contact they had with their birth families and other significant people from their pasts at the time of the interviews. *All the children's adoption orders had been granted, so the contact we explored was exclusively post-order.* We are aware that within the adoption field the term contact has many meanings. For the purpose of this study, however, we were interested in any direct or indirect[4] communication between the children and a range of people

---

2   Children Act 1975, s 26 and now provided for by the Adoption Act 1976, s 51.
3   Children Act 1989, s 2, para 15(1).
4   In this study, direct contact includes face-to-face meetings and communication by letter or telephone. Indirect contact refers to contact via an intermediary.

footnote continued on next page

including birth parents, siblings, extended family members, previous foster carers or others who may have been important in the children's lives.

The issue was explored by asking the children if they were still in contact with any of their birth family members or other important people from their pasts and, if so, to tell us about it; if there was anything about the contact that they wanted to change; and if there was anyone with whom they were not in contact that they wanted to be. These and supplementary questions allowed us to build a picture of the nature of the contact the children were having and gave us insights into their wishes and feelings about it.

FINDINGS

Contact was discussed with 38 of the 41 children. Twenty-four of this sub-sample were having direct or indirect contact with members of their birth families.

Contact with birth parents

Twelve children in the sample have direct contact with their birth parents, usually their birth mother. Three children have letter contact and nine have face-to-face contact. The nature of the contact varies: letter contact is sometimes limited to the receipt of birthday and Christmas cards, and each family's face-to-face contact differs in its context and frequency.

Letter contact
Jackie (aged 8) receives letters and cards from her birth mother on special occasions, via her social worker. Anna (aged 14) also hears from her birth mother through social services, by letter, and explained:

> *I try and write once every month, but now I'm writing more often, because in her last letter she said she would like to hear from me more. So I said, 'Yes'.*

Anna keeps her letters carefully in a drawer and tries not to lose them. Mary

---

4   *continued*
(This classification differs from that used in *Supporting Adoption* (Lowe and Murch, 1999, p.278) in which the term "direct contact" was used to denote only face-to-face contact and indirect contact meant any other form of contact.)

(aged 9) also receives letters, cards and presents from her birth mother, via her social worker, at Easter, Christmas and on her birthday. However, by chance, she also occasionally sees her birth mother and half-siblings, when she goes to the nearby town.

Face-to-face contact

Face-to-face contact is supported by adoptive parents, for instance, by the provision of transport and being present during visits. Most takes place on neutral ground. Ellie (aged 10), for example, meets her birth mother at her adoptive mother's local supermarket and then they go ice-skating, bowling or 'do anything else that comes up'. They usually spend almost a whole day together.

Sue (aged 11) sometimes meets her birth mother at the park. One of her adoptive parents drives her to the meeting. Sue was not sure about the frequency of the contact and suggested that she sees her 'once a month, every three months'. Sue really enjoys the time the time she spends with her birth mother:

> We go for a walk around the park and we've bought some crisps and go out to the ducks and give them cheese-and-onion flavoured crisps or something. Then mum starts telling jokes and I, I can't tell any jokes and we'd all be drunk, feel as though we were drunk by the end of it.

One girl's birth mother lives a few hundred miles away from her adoptive home, and is cared for in a nursing home because she is unwell. Contact is usually arranged in school holidays and the girl and her adoptive mother make visits together. The girl explained:

Girl	I only see her when I feel comfortable about seeing her. She's nice. She's got problems [She is unwell] . . . But I do see her.
Interviewer	So it's when you feel comfortable about it?
Girl	Mainly.
Interviewer	How do you make the arrangement?
Girl	The nurses in the nursing home are really understanding. They're kind and they say, 'When do

> *you want to see her?' ... They don't say, 'You can see her on this date, because that's when we're free'. You can see her when you like.*

Interviewer   *And what do you do when you go and see her?*

Girl   *We talk and talk about my sister, because she doesn't really feel comfortable about seeing her sometimes.*

Interviewer   *So she likes to hear news of your sister through you?*

Girl   *Yes. Sometimes she likes to talk about herself, and she's got friends there. She gets on well with them. She's one of the favourites, you know, with the nurses.*

Two brothers, aged 11 and 9, are visited by their birth parents. They receive separate visits from their birth mother and father, because, as one of them explained, their parents split up several years ago. Both birth parents are welcomed into the adoptive home. One of the boys said their birth father visits quite a lot and had recently taken them out for the day to celebrate his brother's birthday. By contrast their birth mother does not visit very much, just once every two years, but in between her visits they talk to her on the telephone and write to each other. When their birth mother visits, they play and she buys videos for them to watch together.

The children's wishes and feelings about having direct contact with their birth parents

Of the twelve children who have direct contact with their birth parents, six said they were content with the arrangements: at the time of the interview they did not wish to change anything about it. One boy, for instance, does not want to change any of his contact arrangements and explained that it helps him to remember his birth family. Nine-year-old Fiona said that her contact with her birth mother, which includes contact with siblings, made her feel happy, ' 'cause I see them again'. Mary enjoys the letter contact and accidental meetings she has with her birth mother and siblings and has no desire to have any more formal contact with them.

Six children, however, expressed a wish for aspects of their contact to change; five of them wanted to see more of their birth mothers. Melanie (aged 10), for example, who usually sees her mother three times a year, said it felt as though she had not seen her for ages and wanted to see more of her. Andy (aged 11) also sees his birth mother three times a year and did not understand why it was not possible to see her more often. Sue spoke of wanting to see a lot more of her birth mother, explaining matter-of-factly that she likes to see her, '. . . 'Cause she's my Mum'. In between contact, her birth mother occasionally telephones, but Sue cannot initiate contact because, for some reason which she did not explain, she does not have her birth mother's telephone number. Sue felt that if she is not able to have more frequent face-to-face contact with her mother then, as a compromise, she should be able to have her telephone number so they can at least speak more often. Another girl would also like to visit her birth mother, who lives some distance away, more often, although she understands why this is not possible. She explained:

> I'd like it to be more frequent, but I know that can't happen
> because I haven't got many holidays. My [adoptive] mum hasn't
> anyway . . . She has to go to work, so I can't argue with that . . .

In contrast, twelve-year-old Wanda has thoughts about reducing the frequency of her contact with her birth mother. She sometimes struggles to find the time for visits and the demands of her school work come into conflict with her contact arrangements. She said:

> I can't be taken out of school now, 'cause I used to be able to go
> out of school, but I don't want to go out of school now, 'cause I
> want to catch up on my work and I'll just have a pile of
> homework . . . It'll be weekends now . . . She wanted to take me
> out of school, but I didn't want to go out of school.

This conflict of interests may underlie some of her feelings about contact:

> I don't know, sometimes I feel like not seeing them at all.
> Sometimes I have all sorts of feelings.

Two children did not want to change the frequency of contact, but also described how they found aspects of their contact hard to manage. Although one boy said he found the contact with his birth father helpful and was pleased to be able to still communicate with him, he mentioned some painful aspects of his phone contact with his birth mother that he would like to change. He did not say that he wanted the phone contact to stop, but at times finds it upsetting. He said sadly:

> *Yeah. My Mum . . . she can't cope, so if she's fell over and cut herself, she'd be crying down the phone. I wish that could be different. And she's pretty low on the phone. It's like she's worried.*

Janine regarded herself as 'lucky to be able to see my Mum' and said, 'I'm happy with the way things are,' but also spoke of the pain she feels when she and her birth mother part at the end of their contact:

> *Like sometimes when we see [my birth mum] you feel that you need to cry when you leave her and things, but you hold it in to be brave for everyone else . . . I mean it's okay if you get used to holding your tears in, if you know you're going to see your Mum again . . .*

The children's wishes and feelings about not having contact with their birth parents

Twenty-six of the children did not have any contact with their birth parents. Within this sub-sample there were twelve children who, at the time of the interview, were apparently accepting of this, insofar as they said they did not wish for any changes in relation to contact. Seven of the 26, however, explicitly said that they did not want any contact. Another seven of the children expressed a desire to be in contact with one or other or both their birth parents with whom they were not in touch.

When one boy (aged 14) was asked what he felt about not having contact with his birth mother and father, he simply said:

> *I don't mind 'cause I've got my real Mum and Dad here, so I don't need to see them.*

Karen (aged 13) linked her not wanting to see her birth father to his behaviour towards her in the past. She said she did not want to have any contact with him again unless he had changed and explained:

> *But if he's changed and be nice, be really good and sensible then I would be able to contact . . . But if he's not, then I wouldn't. Because after his behaviour, of what he did to me, I don't think I would . . .*

Karen's sister, who was interviewed with her, then asked her what she thought he would do to her if they met. Karen replied emphatically, 'The same thing. I just don't want to see him.' Karen's sister then reassured her that she will not have to see him because he does not know where they live.

John (aged 14) expressed a similar view:

> I often think to myself what they did, I just wouldn't want to see them.

David (aged 12) said that he has no contact with his birth family 'because of the circumstances'. He chose not to elaborate on these circumstances, but added:

> They weren't involved in [the adoption] at all. They just signed the form that we could be given to anybody else and that was it then. We never saw them again. And thank God we didn't.

Of the seven who expressed a desire to be in contact with one or both their birth parents with whom they were not in touch, only Daniel (aged 12) was slightly uncertain about it. He said, hesitantly, 'I'd quite like to see my Mum really . . . but I don't know really'. A girl (aged 15) was clearer that she wants to meet her birth mother, but thinks that she is not old enough yet and will have to wait until she was 18 or 19. Judy (aged 11) said she found it upsetting that she is not allowed to have contact with her birth mother until she is 18. She also wants to be in contact with her birth father whom she has never seen. She said sadly, 'I just didn't know what happened to him'.

Another child (aged 9) was very keen to be in touch with his birth mother and found it difficult to accept his adoptive mother's explanation for the lack of contact. He said he knew the name of the road where his birth mother lived, but did not know the house number. He said he had talked to his adoptive mother about it and she had said:

> Ah well, sorry, but we can't make you get in contact with her, 'cause they don't know what number she lives at . . .

The boy found this explanation unsatisfactory and said, 'I don't know why they just don't ask'. He then asked the interviewer, with what she felt to be some urgency, 'Are you allowed to ask the court if you are allowed to see your parents?'. The interviewer explained that contact is something that is discussed in court and then encouraged him to raise this issue with his social worker who still visits him regularly.

Although Anna is accepting, for the time being, of the letter contact she has with her birth mother, and is pleased to receive the photographs her birth mother sends of her many brothers and sisters, she is also looking forward to meeting her when she is older. Thinking about the prospect of a meeting with her mother makes her feel 'Happy, but a bit scared as well'. In the meantime, she wants to be in touch with her birth father. She said:

> [Sighing] . . . *I don't know how to explain it. If there's people you don't sort of, like, know how they are and everything. 'Cause I have never, ever heard from my Dad and I really wanted to. But I just don't know where to start with it. I've never even talked to Mum about it. But I really do want to get and meet my Dad as well.*

Before moving on, the interviewer then explored the possibility of Anna discussing this with her adoptive mother to whom she felt close. As the interviewer was preparing to leave, her mother told her that Anna had already taken the opportunity talk to her about contact, while her sister was being interviewed.

As well as wanting to see more of her birth mother, another girl also wants to see her birth father whom she has not seen for nine years. She understands that he has decided not to see her because he does not feel comfortable about it. She seems accepting of this decision, saying she does not feel angry with him and that she sees it as 'his choice really'. She is, however, pleased to receive some news of him through a relative with whom she had recently established contact. She explained that she does not know very much about him, but at least she now knows, 'Just things like, where he lives and how he's doing and stuff'. She added:

> *I'd like to know more about my family. I found out quite a lot from her, and it makes me feel like I want to see other people that I hadn't heard of before.*

Another girl, Riahanna (aged 12), is very keen to meet her birth mother when she is older. She said:

> . . . *I kept asking . . . Mum and Dad what the court said. And you know when you're 18 you can move house, but when I'm 18 of course I can go and see my real mum . . . Yes, yes, I definitely do*

*tell my Mum about fifty times that I want to go and see my real
mum. And they said they would sort it out.*

Although Riahanna is only 12, she explained that she and her adoptive
parents have already discussed some of the possible arrangements for
meetings:

*They'll drop me off or they'll put me on a train, whatever, if I
want to. And they said for the first time they need to come with
me . . .*

She hopes eventually to be able to see her birth mother on her own. She
explained that she does not know if she has any new brothers and sisters
and would like the opportunity to find out. She also expressed concern
about her mother's well-being and wants to see her so she can:

*See how my mum is going, 'cause she's sick, not like me, no-one
to help her, as people have helped me.*

Contact with siblings

Twenty-seven of the 41 children have siblings, including half-siblings, from
whom they are separated. Of those, 17 have contact with at least one of
their siblings. As with contact between children and their birth parents,
contact between siblings varies in its frequency and context. Most of the
contact is face-to-face, but for two of the children it is restricted to letter-box
contact.

Face-to-face contact
Luke (aged 9) said he does not see his siblings very often because they live
some distance away from his adoptive home. He explained how his sporadic
contact is organised:

*They don't phone or write to me, but when I want to go to their
house or they want to come here, normally my Mum phones
them up and just asks them . . . I let my Mum know and
sometimes my Mum asks me if I want to see them again. And
most of the time I say, 'Yes'.*

Sophie now has contact with her brother when she sees her birth mother
about once a month and mentioned the fact that, as they have grown older,

the nature of their contact has changed. She said:

> I used to go and play with him. I used to go and stay with him for
> a day and he used to come around mine sometimes. But we
> don't do that anymore because he's 15.

Jocelyn (aged 12) has many siblings and half-siblings who are cared for by several families and are widely dispersed. Social services organise an annual gathering to try to bring the whole birth family together with all their past and present carers and social workers. In between get-togethers, Jocelyn has various types of contact with some of her siblings. She has occasional contact with a brother and sister who are in an adoptive placement together. She sees one of her brothers every third week and sometimes speaks to another brother on the telephone. Jocelyn regularly meets one of her sisters, to whom she feels close, and keeps in touch with her by telephone in between meetings. She said:

> We just talk about what we've been doing over the weeks and if
> we're doing anything in the following week and my sister rings
> me up and she says, 'Would you like to go to the cinema?'. I ask
> my Mum and if she says 'Yeah', we'll like go . . .

Anna and Melanie both have contact with siblings which is limited by the availability of local authority transport. Melanie has contact with her sister when she sees her mother, but used to see her independently until transport was stopped. Anna has siblings living with two families about 40 miles away from her adoptive home. She is no longer able to see them as often as she would like and only has contact on special occasions. She said:

> Sometimes I go and see them, but social services all of a sudden
> stopped us and wouldn't provide the transport. But when I was
> adopted they said they would provide the transport. But now all
> of a sudden they stopped it. So we have to provide some of it . . .

Letter contact with siblings

Thomas (aged 9) has letter contact with one of his half siblings, who lives about 200 miles away from his adoptive home, in the town where Thomas was born. Every Christmas he and his adoptive family send his half-siblings a card and sometimes his mother and half-sister write to each other. However, Thomas said he did not really read the letters himself and it was unclear whether he was interested in their content.

Dione also sends one of her half-siblings Christmas cards. She began to do so after an extraordinary chance first meeting when she was 13. She explained:

> I was with two of my friends in McDonald's and I was eating and this girl came up to me and said, 'Oh, my friend thinks she knows you,' and the person that was her friend came up to me and goes, 'Hello, can I have a word with you for a minute?'. She goes, 'Hello, I think I'm your sister' . . . I didn't even know who she was but she just recognised me.

During their conversation, Dione's sister wrote down her address to enable them to keep in touch and Dione has carefully kept the McDonald's piece of paper on which the address was written. Since then she has met her once more while out shopping.

The children's wishes and feelings about contact with siblings

Six of the 17 children who had contact with at least one sibling wanted to see their brothers and sisters more often. Dione, for instance, said her chance meeting with her half-sister made her feel good and she found it helpful because, 'Like, you know what your actual family look like'. Dione is of mixed-heritage and said she and her sister did not look alike, adding, 'she's got a different dad and he was white, so she's white as well'. She is aware of having several other half-siblings and said, 'I've got a lot, but I don't know who they are,' and 'Well, I'd like to see a lot more of them'.

Anna, whose contact with her siblings was restricted by the availability of local authority transport, was angry with social services. She said they should:

> Keep their promises! Because they broke the promise about us having transport down to see my brothers. So they broke that. . .

Jocelyn's contact arrangements with her siblings and half-siblings are complex and not without difficulties. She was very upset when her contact with a brother and sister who are in an adoptive placement together was temporarily stopped by her brother and sister's new mother and father. Evidently they mistakenly believed that Jocelyn had passed their phone number, against their wishes, to another of her brothers. At the time of the interview she was also upset that she had recently left several messages for her brother and sister on their parents' answering machine, but no-one had responded. Jocelyn has also lost touch with her oldest sister who had recently moved. She thought she might have to wait until the next family barbecue before seeing her again.

Another girl speaks to one of her brothers, to whom she is particularly close, on the phone and visits him about three times a year. They have lived apart for about six years and she said:

> I do miss him. Sometimes I get desperate to see him ... I used to get desperate to see him when I left him and sometimes it's quite upsetting, but I don't get that as much. I don't get that now... I do look forward to seeing him, but I don't, like, get desperate. I get used to it.

Paul (aged 12) was troubled by his limited contact with some of his siblings and his non-existent contact with others and talked about it at some length. He said he was having contact with four of his siblings. He has a younger brother who has been adopted by a family who live close to his adoptive home and Paul regards him as a friend. He saw some advantages to not living with him:

> I like him, 'cause I mean, if you see your sister or brother too much then you end up arguing sometimes, don't you? If you only see them a few times, like twice a month or something, then you get on with them.

However, Paul also has three siblings whom he said he does not see very often. He had visited two of them twice during the previous year and regarded that as 'Well, hardly ever'. He said he gets on well with them when he visits and enjoys playing hide-and-seek with them. He does not write or telephone them in between visits because he does not know their address or telephone number. He had only seen another sibling a few times in the past when she was much younger. When asked if there was anything about his contact with his birth family that he wanted to change, he said he wanted to see all his siblings more:

> At least twice a week. Well, twice every two weeks or something like that. Maybe twice a week.

When asked if he had discussed this with anyone, he said, referring to his adoptive parents:

> No. They probably wouldn't want to. They'll just say, 'Oh yeah, you can see them'. But then they'll get fed up with a few times a week.

He then tried to calculate how many more visits he would have a year if he saw his siblings twice a week rather than twice a year. He then mentioned another sibling who he would like to be in contact with. He said:

Paul	'Cause she went off somewhere else in a family. Don't know anything about her really [sighing].
Interviewer	What sorts of things do you want to know?
Paul	I'll know what they look like and that. 'Cause I don't know what they look like. I don't know what [my third sister] looks like properly. I think she's got the same hair as mine.
Interviewer	Anything else about her you'd like to know?
Paul	How old she is.
Interviewer	Anything else?
Paul	And where she lives. Even if I knew the phone number then that would be a lot better . . . I'm in contact with [my brother] perfectly really, but with my sisters, no.

Later in the interview, Paul mentioned another sibling:

> I've got another brother, but I don't really think about him. He's called Stephen, but I think he still lives with [my birth parents].

The interviewer asked Paul if he felt he wanted to speak to anyone else about his feelings about contact and he said he would speak to his adoptive parent about it. He took the opportunity to begin to do so immediately after the interview. As the interviewer was preparing to leave, Paul asked his adoptive mother if he could see his two sisters again. She explained gently that it would not be possible to see one of them because she did not live with her adoptive parents anymore. This added an unexpected dimension to the issue and Paul's puzzled expression suggested he was having difficulty making sense of the information. His mother commented that she had in fact mentioned this to him before. She repeated that one of his sisters did not live with her adoptive mother anymore and was perhaps living with another foster family. The interviewer sensed that their discussion would continue after she had left.

In contrast to Paul and the other children who wanted to see and hear from their siblings more often, only Simon implied that he might be having a little too much contact with one of his brothers. He mentioned that he sees two of his five siblings and half-siblings. He is pleased to hear from one of them, but finds the other 'a bit of a pain' at times because he rings him frequently about 'just silly things'.

The children's wishes and feelings about not having contact with their birth siblings

Of the ten children who were not having contact with any of their siblings from whom they were separated, two wanted to establish contact with at least one of them. Steve, for example, said that if the practicalities of getting in contact could be overcome, he would like to be in touch with his sister:

> [My brother] *I'm not really too bothered about, but because [my sister] was like, looked after us, me and John, she was the oldest, she took care of me and John, I wouldn't mind seeing her again. But the problem is how to see her. She'd be grown up now. She was much older than us. . . So that's the problem.*

Judy also wanted to be in touch with a half-brother and was almost in tears when she talked about her separation from him. Expressing her loneliness, she said she would like to be in contact because, 'It would give me someone to talk to'.

We assume that six of the children were, at the time of the interview, content not to be in touch with their siblings, insofar as they did not wish to change anything about their lack of it. Only one child, Lucy, made it explicit that she felt relieved not to have contact. There had been conflict in her relationships with them and she said she did not want to see them, ' 'cause I think they would still be horrible to me'.

Contact with previous foster carers

Fifteen of the children have contact with previous foster carers. Without exception the foster carers with whom the children had contact were those who had cared for them immediately before moving to their adoptive homes.

Face-to-face contact

Twelve of the 15 children have face-to-face contact with their foster carers. Seven of them described a pattern to it. Others were hazy about its frequency. Jocelyn sees her foster carer at her birth family's annual get-together and in between meetings speaks to her on the phone. Judy also sees her foster carers once a year, on her birthday, and also has occasional phone and letter contact.

Debbie (aged 10) meets her foster carers twice a year and hears from them on her birthday. Wanda said she visits her foster carers and talks to them 'as much as my brother'. Anna and Paul's foster carers are still caring for some of their siblings and they therefore have contact with them when they visit their siblings: about once a month and twice a month respectively. Unusually, Mary, whose last foster carer was her adoptive mother's mother, has contact with her previous foster mother everyday.

Letter contact

Three of the 15 children have letter contact with their foster carers. Two teenage brothers keep in touch with their foster carers by sending cards and presents and have recently begun to speak to them on the phone to 'have a little chat with them now and again'. One of them explained, 'Usually it's just to say thank you and, like, tell them what we've been up to lately'. Daniel and his foster family sometimes exchange cards, but no longer meet.

The children's wishes and feelings about contact with foster carers

Four of the children expressed their contentment with the contact arrangements with foster carers. Although Judy's foster carers visit her on her birthday, it is her telephone contact with them that she finds especially helpful. She explained that at times she feels lonely and the contact simply gives her someone to talk to. Another girl (aged 12) finds it easier to talk to her foster mother than anybody else and can talk to her about 'anything'. She therefore finds it helpful to be able to talk to her on the telephone when she feels the need to talk to someone.

Both Steve and John also particularly appreciate their telephone contact with their foster carers and suggested that it helps them remember part of their pasts. John explained:

> I think it's quite good to keep in contact because when we were younger we didn't, like, know much about them and, like, how they looked after us when we were younger, what they did for us while we were there . . .

Steve felt he benefits from the contact himself, but also that his foster carers appreciate being able to follow his and John's development. He said of his foster carers:

> I've heard how they looked after me. They're quite special to me . . . They're still very much in the picture. I'd like to keep in touch with them . . . I just sort of like to know them again. Like, they still remember us. They haven't heard our voice for ages. We were just little kids' voices and [when] they actually hear our voices, feel us growing up. I just thought it would be nice to get to know them again . . . So we just phone them up, I enjoy phoning up . . . As soon as I hear [my foster mother's] voice, for some reason just all the memories just flood back into my mind. I can remember things, photographs. I just see them in my head again, and I remember things.

Three other children, however, want to see more of their foster carers. Debbie, for example, said it was good to be in touch with her foster carers so that 'we can hear what's happening'. She would like to see them 'a bit more than we do'. Corine said she would also like to see hers more frequently. Daniel, whose contact at the time of the interview was limited to letters and cards felt he would like to see them a little bit, just to 'see how they're getting on'.

The children's wishes and feelings about not having contact with their foster carers

Of the eight children who said they did not have contact with previous foster carers, we can assume that six of them were content with the situation in so far as they did not express dissatisfaction about it. However, two sisters, Nicky (aged 11) and Lucy (aged 10), talked about their feelings about not being in touch. Nicky described how by chance her adoptive and foster families met in a park one Christmas holiday. They were all invited back to her foster family's holiday home and spent time playing with her foster carers' children. Nicky would like to see them again, '. . . 'cause they were really nice'. Lucy also wants to meet them again and explained:

> I used to invite them to my party . . . but then Mum said I can't invite them again because it was too far for them and they won't come on time . . .

Lucy did, however, also express some conflicting feelings about the possibility of contact with them. She said she felt upset at the thought of seeing them.

Contact with extended birth family

Five children talked about contact with members of their extended birth family. When Andy, for instance, has contact with his siblings, he also visits birth aunts and uncles who are similar ages to himself. Peter (aged 11) also sees a birth aunt and uncle, who live close to his adoptive home, and goes to the same school as some birth cousins. Thomas has occasional contact with his birth father's sister and her husband and enjoys going to stay with them on their farm for weekends.

As with contact with birth parents and siblings and foster carers, some of the contact with extended birth family members is limited by adoptive parents' work commitments and geographical factors. Simon wants to see more of his birth grandparents, but understands that this is not possible because they live a considerable distance from his adoptive home and his adoptive father does not have many days off work to use for travelling to see them. Andy wants to have contact with one of his grandfathers when he has not seen for some time and an uncle who might be difficult to see because he often works away from home.

Contact with previous social workers

Eight children talked about the occasional contact they have with social workers who are no longer allocated to them. Five of the children have face-to-face contact, and three have letter or telephone contact or both. Ian (aged 12) sees the social workers who were involved in his case at an annual party organised by his adoption agency. He said that seeing them gives him a sense that 'they're still looking after us and seeing how we're getting on'.

Simon said his social worker sends him a postcard if she goes on holiday and he sometimes speaks to her, and one of his key-workers, on the telephone. Daniel described the letters he sends to his social worker:

> I don't really say anything personal, apart from what I've done; all the, like, interesting bits I've done since I last wrote to her.

Of the eight children who have contact, five are satisfied with it, but three want more. Sophie visits her social worker about every couple of months and is content with the arrangements. She finds the visits helpful because they give her opportunities to ask her social worker questions about her past and her birth family. Judy, however, wants more contact with her social worker. She is allowed to see and write to her, but is 'not allowed to have real appointments with her'. She feels her limited contact restricts her access to the kind of information Sophie receives from her social worker. When she explained how she felt about this, she mentioned the life story books her social worker is holding for her until she is older. She may have been referring to her social work files or, perhaps, other more sophisticated life story books to add to the one she already has.

> So I can't really find out. But I've got my life story books in her office. When I'm 18, I'm allowed to collect them . . . I just wanted to keep talking to her, but I wasn't allowed to.

Judy understands that she is not allowed any more appointments because her social worker has other people to talk to and other children to look after. She, nevertheless, feels really upset about it.

Two other children who are not in touch with their social workers said they would like to be. David wanted to have contact with his social worker, ''cause he helped a lot'. John mentioned that he had not seen his social worker for over eight years and said, 'Well, it might be nice to see him sometimes'.

Contact with friends from the past

Fourteen children discussed contact with friends, particularly best friends, from previous schools, foster families or residential units. Of those 14, six keep in touch with their friends, usually by writing. The other eight had, with regret, lost touch with important friends. Addresses and telephone numbers had been lost or forgotten and, with the exception of Wanda, the children did not seem to know how they might go about finding them. Wanda had lost touch with the children of one of her foster families and suggested that her social services department holds information which might help her trace them.

SUMMARY

The main points are:

- When talking about contact some of the children expressed feelings of sadness, loss and loneliness, and unveiled their need for knowledge about their birth families and their pasts.
- Almost a third (32 per cent)[5] of the children had post-adoption order contact with birth parents, usually with the birth mother. Most face-to-face contact took place on neutral ground and was supported by adoptive parents with the provision of transport and sometimes their presence during visits. Five of these children were content with the arrangements, but the other seven expressed wishes for aspects of it to change, mostly to see more of their birth mothers. Children without contact expressed a range of wishes and feelings about it. Five children could accept not having contact, or the level of contact they did have for the time being, but mentioned that they hoped to re-establish contact or have more of it when they were older.
- Proportionately more children (63 per cent)[6] had contact with their birth siblings from whom they were separated than contact with their birth parents. However, they similarly expressed a range of views about it. The frequency and context of sibling contact was different for each child and sometimes changed over time.
- Just over a third (37 per cent)[7] of the children had no contact with members of their birth families.

---

5   Based on a sub-sample of 38 children.
6   Based on a sub-sample of 27 children who had siblings, including half-siblings, from whom they were separated.
7   Based on a sub-sample of 38 children.

- Fifteen children had contact with previous foster carers. This provided them with support and links with the past.
- The eight children who had contact with their previous social workers appreciated it because it gave them a sense of still being looked after by them and gave them access to information about their birth families.
- The children did not always understand why it was not possible to have contact, or more contact, with their birth families, or other significant people from their pasts.
- At the time of the interview, in our view, some children were in need of the opportunity to discuss their wishes and feelings about contact with their adoptive parents, social workers or other supportive person.

9   Adoptive Home and School

INTRODUCTION

The data reported in this chapter are about the supportive – or unsupportive – nature of the children's current relationships at home and at school. The material is mainly drawn from answers to some of the exploratory questions asked throughout the Family and Friends exercise[1] and a particular question put to the children at the end of that exercise: 'Of all the people you've put in the picture, who has helped you the most?'. We also use responses to questions about knowing any other adopted people and their openness about being adopted, particularly with teachers and friends at school. When the children were asked about relationships at school, it emerged that some of them had experienced or feared bullying and these findings are recorded at the end of the chapter.

FINDINGS

Relationships with adoptive parents

Thirty-two of the 41 children identified their adoptive parents as sources of support and gave us insights into the helpful nature of their relationships with their adoptive parents. They described five broad categories of help that they particularly appreciate: talking about problems; talking about adoption and the past; being offered comfort and understanding; helping with education and schooling; and, perhaps surprisingly, discipline. Some children mentioned valuing more than one type of help from their parents.

Talking about problems
Ten children said they found their parents supportive because they could talk to them about their fears and troubles. For instance, if Phil (aged 9) is scared about anything, he tells his father who helps him to feel strong again and

---

1   An explanation of this exercise is given in Chapter 2, *Methodology*, p.20.

'not be scared'. Anna (aged 14) said of her adoptive parents:

> They are really, really helpful. Because whenever I've got any
> problems, either with school, with friends, or with any problems,
> then I can always talk to Mum and Dad, but most of the time I
> can't talk to Dad very often, because it's difficult talking to a man
> about your problems [laughing]. But Mum's always there to talk
> to, so we're sort of like best mates in a way. It's really good.

By contrast, two of the girls mentioned seeking support from their fathers
rather than their mothers. One girl (aged 11) said she has arguments with
her adoptive mother. She feels her mother does not understand what she
went through before she was adopted and does not know how she feels.
She said:

> It's really difficult. And she says, 'If you talked to me it would be
> easier'. And I just say, 'I just don't want to talk to you. I just want
> to talk to someone else'.

She added:

> But it has been made easier, because I can talk to my Dad now.

Another girl (aged 10) felt her mother is always too busy to help her or she
will not listen. However, she has a close relationship with her father and she
goes to him for help in sorting out arguments with her siblings and
difficulties she has with friends at school. Her father advises her to 'try to ride
it out' and tells her 'how to work it out'.

Melanie (aged 10) felt she had had to learn to share her troubles with
her adoptive mother and described the turning point in their relationship:

> I ran away before. Yes, because I got told off and I didn't like it.
> So I ran away quite far and I couldn't get back because I didn't
> know my way back . . .

Melanie eventually made her way back home by making friends with
another child whose mother drove her home. She said her adoptive mother
was very upset by her running away and Melanie agreed never to do so
again. Also she said:

> I made a promise to my Mum that if I had any problems then I
> would tell her everything.

Only one child (aged 9) mentioned that she finds it difficult to talk to either of her adoptive parents. She feels scared because they sometimes ignore her when she tries to discuss her worries with them. When she feels ignored, she retreats to her bedroom to be alone. She can, however, discuss her difficulties with her social worker who still visits her regularly.

Talking about adoption and the past

Five children told us that they found their parents particularly helpful when they wanted to talk about their adoptions and pasts. Steve (aged 14), for example, explained:

> I've always been a bit inquisitive about my adoption, what was it like and things like that. And they have answered my questions. And I'm one of those people who likes to know something to do with me that I don't know . . . So if I ask a question about it they wouldn't hesitate in answering it.

Similarly, Paul (12) said of his adoptive parents:

> They tell me about adoption and how I got to be here . . . They have a long sort of conversation about it . . . They got most of the information to me . . . They said why and what happened really.

Ian (aged 12) particularly values being able to talk to his adoptive parents about his past.

> They're kind and you can tell them a lot of things that's happened in the past. If I want to talk to them about serious things they'll listen, and I'll listen. I'll tell them all the stuff and that's a really good thing, 'cause I trust my Mum and Dad.

By contrast, Jocelyn (aged 12), who said she wants to forget the past, appreciates the help her parents give her to do so. She said the topic of adoption 'is not brought up when I'm around. So they try to keep it away from me'.

Comfort and understanding

Four of the younger children in the sample said their adoptive parents helped them by offering them comfort and understanding. For example, Thomas (aged 9) said:

> When I'm upset they make me feel better and let me on their laps
> and talk to me.

Mandy (aged 11) said:

> They all help me, but Mum and Dad try especially hard . . . They,
> like, help me if I break with a friend. They comfort me and say,
> 'The world's not over' .

Another boy (aged 9) said he often feels sad about lots of things, but
particularly about the death of a previous foster carer. When he feels sadness
and grief he goes to his adoptive parents for comfort and he said that they
help him 'to sort things out'.

Help with education and schooling

Eight children said they appreciate the help their adoptive parents give them
with their education. Ian said that his parents had helped him to:

> . . . learn things. Instead of me birth mum and dad, because they
> didn't really learn us anything. I didn't really brush my teeth while
> I was there . . . Writing; reading; spelling; numbers; times tables;
> adds: all sorts of things.

A brother and sister (aged 11 and 12) separately mentioned that they
welcomed their parents' help with their homework.

Fourteen-year-old Simon valued the encouragement his parents give
him to put some effort into his school work. He said they talked to him:

> Well, about careers, how I've got to work hard at school and
> basically get a move on with my work . . . Not just treat it like a
> big joke, like my GCSEs are a long time away. That's what I
> thought when I was in the first year, but it's amazing how time
> has flown on. I can hardly believe that I'm in Year 9 now . . . I
> didn't really take them seriously but now, now I'm actually
> starting to take them a bit more seriously. I can understand what
> [Mum and Dad] meant now. So they've helped.

Discipline

Five children told us that they value discipline from their adoptive parents. Ruth said that she and her sister are silly and naughty sometimes. She explained:

> When we're naughty, they tell us off ... They tell us not to do that again. They don't really say it in a horrible way. They're trying to tell us that if we do something wrong, say sorry and start again, and don't do it next time. Like, telling us what's right and wrong.

Similarly David said of his adoptive parents:

> They tell me the right way to go about things and if I've done something wrong, how to sort it out, things like that.

Relationships with adoptive siblings

Six of the children identified their adoptive siblings as sources of support. Mary (aged 9), for instance, mentioned that she tells her older sister her secrets because she can be trusted not to discuss them with anybody else. Two sisters said they found both their adoptive brothers helpful and one of them suggested that they were 'basically like very good friends'.

Adoptive siblings were more commonly spoken of as people with whom to have fun and fights. For example, nine-year-old Mike enjoys playing football in his back garden with his older adoptive siblings. Mike's birth sister was a little more reserved about them and said:

> They're alright, but sometimes they just bug me and things and say things. But it's alright because I like being called nicknames.

Anna said of her adoptive sister, who is adopted herself:

> [My sister] is very friendly, but she can be a bit annoying sometimes. She's really sweet though and we really, really do get on ... We always do things together. Sometimes you have some little arguments, but we get on really well.

There was some evidence of more strained relationships between other children we interviewed and their adoptive siblings. For example, a twelve-year-old boy was clearly upset by the tension between himself and his

115

younger adoptive sister. He said his sister hits, scratches and pushes him. He added that if he retaliates:

> ... *she puts on this brilliant cry and goes and tells Mum and I get the blame! ... If I tell Mum, she goes, 'Oh, stop being a baby ...'*

He said he finds her behaviour towards him particularly difficult to cope with if he is having 'a stressful time' and wants to be left alone to think. If he then asks her to go away, his sister says, 'Oh, I don't like you; you never do anything'.

Relationships with adoptive extended family

Just two of the children identified members of their extended adoptive families as people who were especially supportive. Mary was in the unusual position of having been adopted by her foster carer's daughter. Her foster carer had therefore become her adoptive maternal grandmother and remained a part of Mary's daily life. Mary had a close relationship with her grandmother who she said had helped her since she was small and was the most helpful person in her life. At the time of the interview, Mary particularly appreciated the support her grandmother gave her with her homework.

One girl (aged 13) spoke of her adoptive cousins as her 'best helpers'. As well as having fun with her cousins, the girl said she is 'able to talk to them quite well'. She talks to one older female cousin in particular and explained:

> *She makes you feel that she wants you to be there and she'll be supportive. But if you're feeling really, really down and she feels you might cry or something, then she might make a little joke about something you've said, even if it's quite serious, which will cheer you up. Well, it cheers me up. I guess it's because she knows I like silly things and she'll cheer me up generally.*

More usually the children who were interviewed spoke about their adoptive extended family members as people who offer them fun. For instance, two brothers talked about enjoying time with one of their uncles who play-fights with them and always gives them sweets. Nicky (aged 11) and Ian mentioned a 'really nice' uncle who plays with them by rolling them around in a big barrel. They also said that they enjoy spending bonfire nights with their grandfather and going to the fair with him.

Relationships with adoptive family friends

Fourteen of the children said their parents' friends were helpful. They described these adults as their godparents, their parents' 'close', 'best', 'good' or 'oldest' friends, or simply as their neighbours. John (aged 14) was specific about the way in which his godparents were helpful, saying, 'they signed the forms to say that Mum and Dad are suitable parents to have us'. Other children felt, like Peter (aged 11), that they were generally 'kind and helpful'. Some of the children enjoyed spending time with their parents' friends and their parents together, going out for meals, celebrating special occasions, or going away on holidays. Others were cared for by these adults after school or while their parents were out working or socialising.

Relationships with other adopted people

Sixteen children told us that they knew children, other than their siblings, who had been adopted. One girl (aged 15) travels to school with a friend who is also adopted and said:

> She told me on the bus once . . . I said, 'Oh, I'm adopted too!'.

Mike is also friendly with a girl in his class who is adopted. He said they sometimes talk about it:

> She doesn't really say much, but she just says '. . . I'm glad about
> Mum and Dad and I'm glad I'm with them because I wanted to
> be with a family'. And I say that as well.

Three of the 16 children who know other adopted children mentioned children who had been adopted by step-parents. Jocelyn found it puzzling that a girl in her class could be adopted yet still live with their birth father. She said:

> One day she came out with that she was adopted. But I don't
> think she is 'cause she said that she still lives with her father, but
> has a new mum. But she says she is, so I think, well, if she says it,
> well, then she must be.

Three children knew teachers who were adopted and two children had adult members of their adoptive families who were also adopted. Unusually Fiona's adoptive family included three other adopted people – her adoptive father, an uncle and a cousin.

Thirteen children talked about the value of knowing other adopted children. Dione said simply, 'It's nice to know other people who are in your situation'. Debbie found it comforting to be aware that there are other adopted children attending her school because it means that she and her sisters are 'not the only ones'. Indeed, David thought he was 'the only one' and was relieved when a teacher told him she was adopted and encouraged him to feel more positive about it.

Sue (aged 11) said it was helpful to know other adopted people, 'Just to share their views on being adopted'. Another girl (aged 13) also explained why she thought it was valuable:

> Maybe on the anniversaries, being able to go up to them and say,
> 'Well, this is the day I went to court,' and for them to know what
> I was talking about. Other people [who hadn't been adopted]
> might think, 'Well, what do you mean?'.

In relation to knowing other adopted people, seven children mentioned attending annual parties organised by their adoption agencies and summer camps arranged by PPIAS (now Adoption UK). The children enjoyed these occasions for the combination of entertainment and spending time with other adopted people. Daniel and Jack were particularly enthusiastic about the camps. They said:

Daniel	Oooh, it's nice. It's good because you know you're not the only one that's been adopted and . . .
Jack	[Enthusiastically interrupting] There're these quizzes.
Daniel	There're these quizzes as well and games and adventure playgrounds and swimming pools and things like that in it. So it's a nice camp site . . .

Relationships with pets

Twenty children mentioned the importance of their pets during the course of their interviews, usually during the Family and Friends exercise and regarded them as 'one of the family'. Phil was particularly close to his dog. He had most fun with him and said:

> Sometimes I read her a story, the dog a story. And just when I

come home from school she lies on my bed and I watch telly with her.

Phil said his dog and cats were 'good' to him and amongst those 'people' who helped him the most. Debbie mentioned finding it helpful to talk to her cat, saying, 'She miaows as if she's talking back'. John described his dog as '. . . the friendliest thing on four legs'.

SCHOOL

Openness about being adopted

Thirty-three of the 41 children talked to us about the extent to which they were open with friends and other children at school about being adopted. Their experiences fell within four broad categories of openness. Some children did not want anybody to know; others told a few select friends; others told all their friends; and others were in a position of everyone in their year or school knowing.

Within all categories of openness, there were children who did not have full control over whether they told other children, because it was obvious to others that there was something unusual about their circumstances. Children in transracial placements, for instance, may be more easily identified as being adopted than children in same-race placements. All Dione's friends knew that she was adopted because she had told them herself, but she also thought they had worked it out for themselves because, 'I'm coloured and my Mum and Dad are white'. When another girl first moved to her adoptive home, she met a neighbour who was going to the same school as her. This neighbour asked her, '. . . how come I'd moved, just me?' and the girl felt that she had to tell her that she was adopted.

Children who did not want other children to know that they were adopted

Four of the 33 children did not want any other children to know that they were adopted. Judy, for example, regarded her adoption as her 'personal business'. Debbie was sometimes asked if she was adopted, because she and one of her siblings look very different, and she has chosen to deny it. She said that she does not want to tell people because they will 'go spreading it around'.

Similarly, Sophie (aged 12) feared that, if she told anyone, before long everyone in her school would know. She said emphatically, 'None of my friends will ever know'. When Mary (aged 9) was asked if she tells other children that she is adopted replied, 'You must be kidding! I don't tell anybody'. Her advice was:

> If you're a child and you're going to be adopted, you shouldn't
> tell anyone because if you tell them, nobody'll respect you.

Children who told a few selected friends

Thirteen of the 33 children only told a few selected friends that they were adopted. Several of them expressed fears which were similar to those of children who do not tell anybody. They were worried that knowledge of their adoption would spread uncontrollably. They also feared being questioned about it. Peter had only told one or two friends and said:

> They were the kind of people who keep it under their hat: they
> don't go spreading it around the school.

John explained how he decides which friends to tell:

> I tell the ones which have been friends with me the most. The
> ones that aren't likely to break friends and go and tell other
> people.

He described what he tells them:

> Well I don't tell them much. I don't tell them all the personal
> things . . . I just tell that I was adopted. I told them that I used to
> live in Nottingham and now I come over here, Sheffield. They don't
> pressure me or anything. I told them that and they left it.

One boy tells his friends, in the hope of pre-empting their questions, but only those he regards as the 'kindest and nicest'. Another girl only discusses her adoption with friends who she thinks will understand.

Lucy has told a few of her friends and asked them to keep it a secret. Sue has also only shared it with one of her closest friends who has kept her promise not to tell anyone. Sue described telling her:

> I just told her quickly, asked her, made her swear that she
> wouldn't tell anyone . . . and then ran off. And she started

chasing me, going, 'Sue, why are you running off? It's nothing to be embarrassed about'.

Only Anna's really close friends at school know that she is adopted and she regards it as a secret. At her previous school she had, however, discussed it with her small tutor group. Her tutor had asked members of the group to think about their deepest secret and suggested that, if they felt able, they should 'let it out'.

Anna did not say whether she was given any assurances from the group about confidentiality, but said:

So I did. So I goes, 'Well, I'm adopted and that's my deepest secret'. And everyone went, 'Oh'.

She thought other members of the group were a little shocked. They then asked her a few questions about the time she was living with her 'real Mum and Dad'. She said that in retrospect she did not mind telling them.

John (aged 14) had recently had a conversation with his closest friends about being adopted. He said they were inquisitive about what it was like and because they are good friends he did not hesitate to answer their questions. He commented:

It was pretty hard for them to accept that I'd been adopted. They thought that I was a normal boy with [siblings], Mum and Dad and as soon as the news was broken to them that I was adopted, they just couldn't believe it. They refused to believe it. Then when they asked me the questions and I was answering them. It took a lot of convincing from me . . .

Another child (aged 14) similarly made the point that even when children were bold enough to say they have been adopted, they were not necessarily believed. She suggested that this was because 'some children say they've been adopted to get attention'. She values having her life story book as her proof that she has been adopted.

Children who told all their friends about being adopted
Four of the 33 children told all their friends that they were adopted. Simon (aged 14) said he did not mind telling anyone that he got to know because he was not ashamed of it. It was perhaps fortunate that Mary felt strongly that they should know, because the issue was raised during an exercise in

class about families. Mary said:

> They were on about families and all that. And they said on the
> questions, 'Are you adopted?'. Me and Jane are sharing a piece
> of paper and I go, 'I'm adopted'. And she goes, 'Are you?' and I
> go, 'Yeah' . . . And you had to read your piece of paper out . . .
> and tell everybody your answer.

Chantelle said some of her school friends were surprised to learn that she
was adopted, but did not ask her about it afterwards.

Children who were in a position of everyone in their year or school knowing that they were adopted

Twelve of the 33 children were in the position of all the other children in their
year or school knowing that they were adopted. Phil said that all the children
in his school knew because he had told them. Another boy, Mark (aged 11),
mentioned it to one boy and soon afterwards everybody seemed to know,
but he did not mind them knowing.

Ruth (aged 11) similarly described how she had told one friend and
'now everyone seems to know' and feels 'sort of good' that they know. She
likes to be asked about it. Daniel was even more positive about people
knowing. He said:

> It's quite fun being adopted really, because you can tell people
> that you've been adopted. I'm not really embarrassed about
> being adopted – talking to people about it. And now nearly
> everyone in my year knows I'm adopted, but they don't make fun
> of me or anything . . . some people think I'm quite lucky to be
> adopted really.

Wanda (aged 12) also advocated openness with other children:

> I think its better to be open because you find you can let it out.
> Sometimes, if you keep adoption to yourself . . . it's your choice
> really, but the emotion will be stuck there. So it's better to let it
> out and let other people know if you want to.

David had wanted to be open about his adoption with other children at
school, but said the following:

David   *I found it difficult to tell people that I was adopted when I first came to this school and there were some bad rumours going round . . . But I told them the truth and how it all happened.*

Interviewer   *What kind of bad rumours were going round?*

David   *Well, adopted people were really nasty and nobody liked them.*

Three other children were also troubled by other children's awareness of them being adopted. Mike, for instance, explained:

Mike   *In my class there's another person who's adopted and he didn't like talking about it. A bit like me as well sometimes. Some people push us dead hard to answer questions about it that we don't want to.*

Interviewer   *What sorts of questions do they ask?*

Mike   *Like, 'Are you adopted? Are you adopted?'. And they keep on coming round saying, 'Are you adopted? Are you adopted?'. And sometimes I just don't want to tell them because I don't want to share it with them . . . But they keep on pushing, 'Go on. Go on'. And I keep on saying, 'No' and 'I don't like it'.*

Mike added that he did not know why they were so interested.

Openness with teachers

Thirty-two children told us whether one or more of their teachers knew that they were adopted. Twenty-eight of them thought their teachers did know and four said that they did not. Fourteen children were unclear who had informed their teachers. Eleven said that their adoptive parents had told them, and only three children had done so themselves.

While most of these 28 children did not discuss their adoptions with their teachers, ten children described how certain teachers had been especially supportive in relation to their adoptions. Thomas, for example, said he used to get upset when his adoption was 'going on' and he found it was good to talk to two particular teachers. He valued the knowledge that one of them had had personal experience of the adoption process by adopting two boys, 'so she knew what it was like'.

Janine also had a teacher, her form tutor, who helped her through the process by being 'very supportive and protective'.

> *When I was going through the actual procedure she was quite*
> *supportive when I needed to talk to her. If I was feeling down she*
> *was quite happy to stay behind at lunch time or break time, if the*
> *room was empty, and talk to me . . . If anything happened, like,*
> *when I found out* [my brother] *was being adopted , or when the*
> *social worker was coming that evening and I was feeling*
> *particularly down in the dumps, then I used to say, 'Well, do you*
> *mind if I talk to you?'. And she'd talk to me.*

This teacher helped by listening and talking to her like a friend. She always asked Janine to let know her know how her adoption was progressing and said she hoped that everything would go well.

Another girl (aged 11) had a special needs teacher whom she talked to quite often about her adoption. This girl spoke to her particularly when she was feeling misunderstood by her adoptive mother. She explained that her teacher:

> *. . . keeps secrets and things. 'Cause you know that she won't tell*
> *anyone or anything. Yes, you can trust her . . .*

She sometimes felt that she wanted to move again and her teacher tried to calm her down. The teacher encouraged her to accept her situation by saying, 'You're here now and you can't move,' and suggested that she should do as she is told at home to try to make life easier for herself. The girl found this really helpful and felt that this teacher understood what she had been through in her life.

Simon (aged 14) talked about two primary school teachers who had been especially supportive through many difficult times. He said:

> *In junior school I wasn't one of those very well behaved kids, I*
> *was a bit of a mischief-maker. And they helped me when I got*
> *into trouble, they kind of bailed me out, and I really like them . . .*
> *They said good things about me and spoke to me and made me*
> *feel a lot better . . . If I was in trouble with* [one teacher], *say,*
> *they'd say, 'He isn't really that bad,' and to give me another*
> *chance . . . They were firm with me, but in a nice kind of way . . .*

They really encouraged me to work harder and, as I was saying, they wouldn't shout at you . . .

He also had a secondary school teacher whom he went to for help. Simon described how he had recently had quite a bad row with his adoptive mother over watching a late television programme without her permission. He said, 'She got cross and I got cross and everything just got from bad to worse'. Simon went to his teacher for some advice:

She told me what to do . . . I went home and did it and things just started to get better after that . . . [She] advised me to just stay calm. So when I got home I apologised to Mum and I understood 'cause [my teacher] said, 'You must understand that she'll still be a little cross with you, but not to really take it to heart'. And what she said really helped . . . Those things kept going through my mind . . . So, she's a real miracle worker, sorting out problems.

In contrast, two children had chosen not to discuss difficulties relating to their adoptions with their teachers. One boy said:

I don't really want to talk to the teachers because they don't really know much about it.

Another boy felt too scared to confide in his teacher. Although he had at times wanted to talk to his teacher about his adoption, he stopped himself because he thought he would be told off and that his teacher was:

. . . sometimes a bit nasty as well, a bit loud, and I thought he was going to shout at me or something.

Bullying

Although we did not raise the subject of bullying, during the course of the interviews, 13 children described being verbally harassed or physically attacked or both by their peers. Ten of the 13 children mentioned having 'the mickey taken out' of them, being made fun of, and being teased by other children at school. The other three children had been physically hurt by other children. Six of the 13 children attributed this bullying directly to other children's knowledge of them being adopted. Three others thought they were victims because they were in some way 'different'.

Paul was one of the children who said other children made fun of him sometimes because he was adopted. He said people think he is different to everybody else. They sometimes stare at him and whisper. He added:

They go, 'Oh, he's adopted'. That's it really. 'He's adopted'. But of course they don't know the real story behind it all.

When asked about the effect this has on him, Paul said he finds it hurtful. Although he is getting used to it, he tries to 'suck in' his feelings about it. He had recently asked for help from his adoptive parents about how to cope with it.

Steve also thought that some of the verbal harassment he has been subjected to at school is directly attributable to him having been adopted. He said the other children put him down because they think, 'You're different from the rest of us because you haven't say got a proper mum and dad'. He described one particular incident when he said one boy was really getting at him:

He'd been eavesdropping a lot when me and [my friend] *were talking* [about my adoption]. *He was really taking the mickey and that really got me mad. I really did have to stop myself hitting him. I was afraid maybe he'd spread it around and have the whole school, like, all talking about it, getting on my nerves about it. And I can't exactly take on the whole school, can I?* [Laughing]

Judy was not so sure that the bullying she suffered was anything to do with her being adopted. At first she said she was picked on and sometimes bullied because 'it seems I'm just different'. Then she pondered over the possibility that there might be some connection:

I'm not sure really. My friend told me when I first came to this school, that I'm at now, they said, 'Oh, I don't like her 'cause she's adopted,' and it made me pretty sad.

Of the three children who had been physically hurt, two of them linked the bullying with being adopted. One child had had her head bashed by some older boys in school. Another keeps being kicked as her attackers chant:

Ha, ha, ha. Ha, ha, ha, that I'm adopted.

The third child who had been physically attacked had recently been stoned by two boys at school in the playground. Phil showed the interviewer his scars from the attack and said he had since been hurt in other ways:

> Well, playing football with some of my friends . . . and I always play football there and they kicked me in the belly and I went up against the wall and banged my head.

He had also been threatened. When the interviewer asked him about the nature of the threats, he went pale and said, 'No comment'. The boy did not, however, say anything to suggest that he associated his victimisation with his adoption.

Dealing with bullying

Five of the thirteen children who said that they had experienced bullying tried to deal with it with the help of teachers. Phil, for instance, gave the stones his attackers had used to his form teacher, who then reported the incident to a staff meeting. Although Daniel did not have any personal experience of being bullied because of his adoption, he knew, if it happened, that he would seek support from his teachers:

> And if any one does start picking on me, about being adopted, my Head of Year sorts it out because she's . . . very strict about those things. And she thinks you shouldn't make fun of people like that.

Judy and Phil described in detail the behaviour management and anti-bullying policies that operate in their schools. Phil said:

> At our school if you're naughty, you get put on a card like football. You won't go out on the yard . . . Say if you get a yellow card, for instance, you're not allowed out for a week 'cause you're doing detention. If you get a red card, you do two weeks in detention and a letter goes home to your parents.

Judy felt her school's behaviour management code had effectively stopped the bullying to which she had been subjected. Phil's school's bullying policy was used to try to deal with the two boys who had stoned and kicked him and the boys were put on red cards and spoken to by the headmaster. However, at the time of the interview, the bullying was continuing and his adoptive father was trying to protect him by arranging for him to be taught

127

at home. Phil explained:

> It would stop me being bullied. And I wouldn't need to walk
> home because they bully me then.

Other children had different strategies for dealing with bullying. Ruth and her friends 'stick up' for one another if any of them are in any trouble with bullies. She said, 'We're all like a gang and we all help each other'. Simon had another approach and said, 'I just don't listen to them'. John said he tried not to be bothered by what they say.

Vulnerability

Mandy made a comment which recognises that the effect of bullying depends on the vulnerability of the person being victimised. She said that she feels that her life experiences mean that she finds bullying particularly upsetting. If she is bullied, she needs people to understand that she had 'been through a lot of things' and may respond by being more upset than other children.

SUMMARY

The main points in this chapter are:

Home

- Over three-quarters (78 per cent) of the children identified their adoptive parents as sources of support. They described five ways in which they are particularly helpful: talking about problems; talking about adoption and the past; offering comfort and understanding; helping with education and school; and giving discipline. Some children valued more than one type of help from their parents.
- A few children (20 per cent) found their adoptive siblings and extended adoptive family members helpful, but they were more commonly spoken of as people with whom to have fun and fights.
- About a third (34 per cent) of the children said their parents' friends were helpful, enjoyed socialising with them and being cared for by them in their adoptive parents' absence.

- Forty per cent of the sample knew other people, excluding their siblings, adoptive family members and teachers, who were also adopted. These relationships decreased their sense of 'being the only one'.
- Pets as sources of comfort and companionship were important members of the family for half (49 per cent) the children.

School

- About half (52 per cent)[2] a sub-sample of children did not want any other children to know they were adopted or only wanted a few trusted friends to know, fearing that this information about themselves would be 'spread around'. Underlying the fear of people knowing were other worries about being questioned about it; not being believed; or not being respected. The children did not, however, always have full control over the information themselves and a few children's fears had been realised.
- The other half (48 per cent) of this sub-sample advocated more openness: they told all their friends and did not mind other children knowing that they were adopted.
- Most children (88 per cent)[3] thought their teachers knew they were adopted, although they were not always clear who had informed them. While most (69 per cent) of these children did not discuss their adoption with their teachers, some teachers had been especially supportive. By listening and talking to the children these teachers helped them through the legal process and to resolve difficulties with their adoptive parents.
- Approximately a third (32 per cent) of the sample described being bullied by other children at school. Most of them thought the bullying was directly related to other children's knowledge of them being adopted or them being in some way 'different'. They tried to deal with it by seeking help from teachers (who sometimes enforced behaviour management and anti-bullying policies), friends, or, if the attacks were verbal, trying to ignore them.

---

2   Based on a sub-sample of 33 cases.
3   Based on a sub-sample of 32 cases.

10 Conclusion

INTRODUCTION

This study focuses on a number of crucial issues for older adopted children, including their preparation for placement, settling into the adoptive home, and coping with changes of school, the court process, and the maintenance of links with their birth relatives and their pasts. This final chapter summarises the main messages from the children themselves for adoption policy and practice[1] and links these with the conclusions of the *Supporting Adoption* study (Lowe and Murch, 1999) from which the children's sample was drawn. As pointed out in Chapter 1,[2] to appreciate what the experience of adoption means to the children themselves it is valuable to try to understand children's perceptions in their own language. To do otherwise risks obscuring children's views with too much adult comment and interpretation. In this respect this study is in line with a small but growing body of child related studies (Butler and Williamson, 1994; Moore, Sixsmith and Knowles, 1996; Neale, Wade and Smart, 1998; Masson and Oakley, 1999).

The sample of 41 older adopted children essentially presents an optimistic picture of their adoptive placements. Although some of them expressed anxieties about their pasts, concerns about their contact arrangements, and feelings of being different to their peers because of their adoptions, overall they spoke positively about having been adopted, particularly valuing the support of their adoptive parents.[3] However, it should be remembered that these findings, and their messages for policy and practice, come from interviews with older adopted children whose placements were ongoing. This study does not include the views and

---

1 These should be of interest to policy makers, as well as social work practitioners, foster and community carers and adoptive parents. Some of the messages for practice are particularly relevant to professionals in the family justice and education systems who come into contact with older adopted children.

2 Chapter 1: *Background to the Research*, pp.1–2.

3 See Chapter 9: *Adoptive Home and School*.

experiences of children and young people whose placements have disrupted, or those whose placements were perceived by their parents to be in difficulty when they were invited to take part.[4]

SPEAKING AND LISTENING TO CHILDREN AND INVOLVING THEM IN THE ADOPTION PROCESS

The overarching message of this study is that practice should be sensitive to children's needs, particularly by involving them and keeping them informed in a manner appropriate to their age and understanding, and taking account of their sense of time.

All the support offered directly to older children by adults as they move through the adoption process and settle with their adoptive families needs to be underpinned by good adult–child and child–adult communication. It is the adults who carry the responsibility for trying to establish effective communication. Only through adaptable approaches to communication with the children can the adoption process be sensitive to their very individual needs.

In the development and use of our own research tools, we invested much time and effort in trying to overcome as many of the possible barriers to effective communication with children as possible.[5] We tried to be aware of the differences in age, gender, ethnicity, first languages, social class, and sub-cultures in childhood, for instance, which can all have an impact on communication with children. We also considered how the children's emotional and educational special needs, and disabilities, may also have an effect.

From our direct experience of communicating with older adopted children during the interviews, and the views the children themselves expressed about their understanding of adoption, life story work and contact issues, we learnt that it is particularly important for adults to:

- Express themselves simply and clearly and use concepts which are familiar to the children.

---

4   See Chapter 1: *Background to the Research*, pp.4–5, and Chapter 2: *Methodology*, pp.8-9.

5   Chapter 2: *Methodology*.

- Match their explanations of new ideas to the children's age and levels of understanding.
- Be aware of the possible impact of emotional distress on children's understanding.[6]
- Elicit children's fears and offer reassurances.[7]
- Allow children plenty of opportunities for asking questions.
- Ask children for feedback to see if information and explanations have been remembered and understood.
- Repeat, simplify, expand, or build on explanations if appropriate.
- Use communication tools such as games, prompt cards, books, videos and so on.

It was difficult for the children to remember whether they had had opportunities to express their wishes and feelings about their placements to professionals during the adoption process. We also found it hard to establish the degree to which they felt their views had been taken into account in the subsequent decision-making. However, we were particularly struck by the openness and clarity with which many of the children were able to speak about their past and present wishes and feelings about their placements.[8] Many of them clearly demonstrated their competence to participate in decision-making processes.

We believe that the care we took over four particular aspects of the project had a positive effect on the children's openness:

- introducing ourselves and the project, by using a project leaflet and complementary audio-tape;
- the child-friendly tools we used during the interview, such as the prompt cards;
- our assurances about confidentiality and the safe storage of information; and
- giving children the power to influence important aspects of the interview.

It seems vital that professionals have or learn the skills to communicate effectively with children, not just in relation to adoption work but in respect

---

6 See Brodzinsky (1984).
7 See Waterhouse (1992).
8 See Chapter 1, *Background to the Research*, pp.5–6.

of the whole range of child-related legal and social work practice. Indeed, unless they do acquire and use these skills, the legal requirement under s 6 of the Adoption Act 1976 to 'ascertain [so far as practicable] the wishes and feelings of the child regarding the [adoption] and give due consideration to them, having regard to his age and understanding' cannot really be complied with.[9]

COPING WITH CHANGE

Matching and introductions
With a few exceptions, the children felt excluded from the general process of being matched and introduced to their adoptive family.[10] In particular they did not feel included in the preparation or presentation about themselves for their families. Over half the sample had painfully long periods between being introduced to the idea of adoption and being matched.[11]

Moving home and changing school
The children's comments about their moves to their adoptive homes were particularly poignant. Their descriptions conveyed a sense of isolation and loneliness. They described how these moves meant significant, simultaneous changes in almost every aspect of their lives – a new family, home, neighbourhood, school and friends. It is perhaps surprising that none of them mentioned new names in this context. Despite introductory pre-placement visits, they spoke of the strangeness of their new relationships and environments, and the many adjustments they had to make. The children remembered their early days in their new placements as puzzling and stressful. Some children also had clear memories of difficulties in their new relationships. Many found the change of school particularly testing.[12]

---

9 The same argument applies to all legal proceedings to which the court is directed to ascertain and consider the wishes and feelings of the child, for example, by the Children Act 1989, s 1(3)(a) and, more generally by Article 12 of the United Nations Convention on the Rights of the Child 1989.

10 Chapter 4, *Matching and Introductions*, pp.37–39.

11 Chapter 4, *Matching and Introductions*, pp.39–40.

12 See Chapter 5, *Moving*, pp.62–63 and Chapter 9, *Adoptive Home and School*, pp.119–128.

The findings suggest that there are a number of ways in which children can be supported and helped to cope with all the changes associated with their moves:

- The moves to the adoptive family and the new school can be traumatic and it is vital that the child receives constant reassurances and encouragement from their adoptive parents, previous foster carers and social workers.[13]
- For some children changes happened too slowly, yet for others they were too quick. It is important to try to match the pace of change to the individual child's pace of change.[14]
- Consideration needs to be given to the feasibility of moves taking place during school holidays, to give the children a chance to make adjustments at home before they also have to cope with a change of school. Changing schools needs to be acknowledged as an additional major change in the children's lives.[15]
- Professionals, carers and new family members need to recognise and respect the value of the children's treasured toys and possessions. Some of these can help the children to combat some of their feelings of insecurity at the time of the move and as they settle into their placements.[16]
- Adopters can help by continuing with the children's routines and diets from their foster or community placements for a while and introduce any changes which suit them gradually.
- Adopters can help by welcoming the child into their homes with presents and newly decorated bedrooms.

---

13 See Chapter 5, *Moving*, pp.55–57 and 62–63.
14 See Chapter 5, *Moving*, pp.55–57 and *Supporting Adoption* (Lowe and Murch, 1999), Chapter 20, para 3.3.
15 See also the important findings covering schooling in *Supporting Adoption* (Lowe and Murch, 1999), Chapter 11, paras 3 and 4.
16 See Chapter 5, *Moving*, pp.57–59.

COURT

Many children had particularly clear memories of going to court and remembered finding the idea of having to go to be frightening and worrying.[17] They had fantasies about formidable judges; associations between having to go to court and wrong-doing; fears that the order would not be granted, and uncertainties about the nature of proceedings and their own role in them. Social workers' and adoptive parents' verbal reassurances about having to go to court did not always allay their pre-court fears. (Although some children had had guardians *ad litem*, none of them mentioned their guardians in relation to their preparation for court).

The reality of having to go to court, however, was rarely as frightening as the thought of having to go and often the occasion was valued for the outcome of the proceedings. The children also enjoyed their family celebrations after the court hearings and on anniversaries of their "adoption days".[18]

In professional circles, children's attendance at court hearings is a contentious issue. Irrespective of whether they attend, children need clear information about the court's role in adoption and the nature of the court proceedings. If children do attend court, they need careful preparation.[19]

- There is a need for the development of a wide range of tools to help with the task of explaining the legal process. Tools are needed for different levels of understanding, using various media, such as leaflets, books, videos, audio-tapes and CD-ROMs. As far as we are aware, none are widely available.[20]
- Adoptive families, including the children, need to be offered an opportunity to visit the court building in advance of the hearing. Such visits would allow the children to become familiar with the

---

17 See Chapter 6, *Court*, pp.67–69. The children's fears in this respect mirrored the anxieties reported by many adoptors, see *Supporting Adoption* (Lowe and Murch, 1999), Chapter 13, para 2.3.

18 See Chapter 6, *Court*, pp76–79. See also *Supporting Adoption* (Lowe and Murch, 1999), Chapter 13, para 2.3.

19 See *Supporting Adoption* (Lowe and Murch, 1999), Chapter 13, para 4.

20 The preparation of children to give evidence in criminal proceedings has been greatly helped in recent years by the development and use of resources such as the Child Witness Pack (NSPCC and Childline, 1993) and the availability of books such as Bray's *Susie and the Wise Hedgehog Go to Court*.

journeys from home and the court buildings, waiting and refreshment areas, and toilet facilities.

- There may be a role for a professional worker who specialises in the preparation of children for court, who knows the local court's arrangements and regulations.[21]
- Children need to be asked in advance of the hearing whether they want their judge to wear his or her wig and gown, and their wishes could be communicated to the judge via his or her clerk.
- There is a clear need for a ritual ceremony to mark the making of the adoption order.[22] But as an alternative to the court marking this milestone, consideration could be given to extending the role of the registrar of births, deaths and marriages to include the conduct of adoption ceremonies. Such ceremonies could be held in child-friendly environments, with a simple form of words, concluding perhaps with the issuing of certificates for the children.[23]

LINKS WITH THE PAST

The children were asked about two ways in which they were helped to make sense of, and to maintain links with, their pasts: life story work and contact.

Life story work

Not all the children in the sample had done life story work resulting in life story books, 20 per cent saying they had not[24] – a figure which broadly matched the findings in *Supporting Adoption*.[25] The findings of both studies indicate that agency practice has to improve considerably if it is to meet

---

21 The obvious candidate is a guardian *ad litem*. However, there are already professionals who specialise in the preparation of children for criminal proceedings – preparing children for adoption proceedings could be added to their brief.

22 See Chapter 6, *Court*, pp.75–79.

23 See also *Pathways to Adoption* (Murch *et al*, 1993), p.183.

24 See Chapter 7, *Life Story Work*, p.82.

25 See *Supporting Adoption* (Lowe and Murch, 1999), Chapter 9, para 2.3, which found that almost a quarter of families approved by statutory agencies claimed that their child had no life story book.

criteria for good practice set out in the Social Services Inspectorate's Report *For Children's Sake* (1996). Amongst other things, this requires that:

> *Specific work is done with children which helps secure for them both an understanding and a record about their circumstances and their origins.*

The majority of children who had life story books felt positive about them. Most found them helpful because, as intended, they helped them to understand their pasts and hold on to the threads of their family and placement histories. They appreciated them being kept in easily accessible places and looked at them repeatedly, though because some were mere scrap books it seemed unlikely that they would survive intact for long.[26]

A few children said, or demonstrated, that they did not understand or retain all the information contained in their books, or conveyed to them during the life story work itself.

It is important that professionals and adoptive parents are therefore aware that:

- Life story books need to be physically robust to withstand being looked at time after time.
- Ideally life story work needs to incorporate planning for the revision and updating of the work by adoptive parents and professionals. All available relevant information needs to be periodically reappraised. Any new information needs to be integrated gradually into life story work, in the light of a child's developing understanding of their adoption and changing levels of interest in it.[27]

---

26   See Chapter 7, *Life Story Work*, pp.81–82.
27   See also Ryburn (1992), p.20.

Contact

Almost two thirds (63 per cent) of the children in the sample had some form of contact with their birth family.[28]

When talking about contact, some of the children expressed feelings of sadness, loss and loneliness, and revealed their need for knowledge about their birth families and their pasts. Overall, the children had clear views about the post-adoption-order contact they did or did not have with their birth family members and other people from their pasts. They expressed a whole range of wishes and feelings about it. Of those children who had contact with their birth relatives, some were content with the current arrangements. There were other children who accepted not having contact. Others mentioned that when they were older they hoped to re-establish contact, or have more of it. Some children, however, wanted immediate changes to aspects of their contact. They usually wanted to see more of their birth family members, particularly their mothers and siblings.

Some children were mystified by a lack of, or limited, contact with their birth family members, particularly birth mothers and siblings, or other important people from their pasts, notably foster carers. We were concerned that, at the time of the interview, some children indicated a strong need to talk about their feelings about contact with their adoptive parents or another supportive person. Some of them talked to their parents about contact immediately after the interview, in the presence of the interviewer, and their parents seemed keen to respond.

As observed in *Supporting Adoption* (Lowe and Murch, 1999)[29] the issue of contact has to be governed by the welfare of individual children, including taking into account the children's own wishes and feelings, which may change over the course of time. Those who support older adopted children therefore need to:

- Be aware that the children have powerful and changing wishes and feelings about their contact arrangements which need to be

---

28 See Chapter 8, *Contact*, p.109. This corresponds closely to the findings of the *Supporting Adoption* study (Lowe and Murch, 1999),Chapter 15, para 2, which found that 77 per cent of the parents indicated that their child had some form of ongoing contact with a birth relative.

29 See Chapter 15, para 5.

taken into account in the relevant decision making. Arrangements need to be kept under review.

- Create continuing opportunities for the children to express their changing wishes and feelings about their contact arrangements. Although children may not openly ask for information and explanations about it, this does not necessarily mean that they have no interest in contact with their birth families or other significant people from their pasts.[30]

STIGMATISATION AND BULLYING

Almost a third (32 per cent) of the children in the sample described being bullied at school[31] and sometimes related this to other children knowing that they were adopted and that they were therefore in some way different.[32]

Some children felt strongly that they did not want any other children, or only a few trusted friends, to know that they were adopted. However, they did not always feel they had much control over the information themselves.

Older adopted children can be helped to cope with the stigma of adoption and bullying in a number of ways:

- When matching, social workers need to take into consideration how obvious it will be to others that the children will not be living with their birth parents, how the children may cope with this and what support they might need.
- Adopters and professionals need to be sensitive to children's individual feelings about others knowing that they are adopted.[33] It is important for children to have a feeling of some control over the information about their adoptive status and they should therefore be involved in the decisions about the dissemination of the information. Those children who do not wish to be open about

---

30 See also Sachdev (1991).
31 See Chapter 9, *Adoptive Home and School*.
32 For other findings concerning the pattern of bullying and teasing at school see *Supporting Adoption* (Lowe and Murch, 1999) Chapter 11, para 3.1.
33 This is particularly relevant when considering transracial placements. See also Ince (1998).

their adoptions need to have their desire for privacy acknowledged and respected. Children may need help to develop a brief "cover" story, which is not too revealing and which they can use to explain to others why they are not living with their birth parents.

- To lessen their sense of being "the only one", children need to be given opportunities to share their experiences of adoption with other adopted children and adults.
- Adoptive parents and teachers need to be aware that adopted children are potentially vulnerable to bullying. Schools can support children by promoting an ethos that makes bullying unacceptable and enforcing anti-bullying policies.

THE FINAL WORD

It seems appropriate to end this study by allowing some of the children to speak once again for themselves, with some of their own messages specifically for social work practitioners:

[Social workers] *could try to make the speed a bit quicker for everyone.*

They should try to let their children speak a bit more, so they're not keeping everything stuck inside them.

[Social workers] *could try and see you a little more often or for slightly more time when they come.*

Explain to the children what's going on. Like, give them information about their parents, birth parents, foster parents . . . And, oh, really help them understand what's going on. Encourage the parents to talk about it a bit more. Let the children talk to friends about it.

Understand the child . . . I know they would have to know a lot about the child. To know a lot about them could really help. Spend time with them.

References

Bouchier, P., Lambert, L., and Triseliotis, J. (1991) *Parting with a Child for Adoption: The mother's perspective*, BAAF.

Brodzinsky, D. M. (1984) 'New perspectives on adoption revelation', in *Adoption & Fostering* 8:2, pp.27–32.

Burch, M. (1992) *I Want to Make a Life Story*, National Foster Care Association.

Butler, I. and Williamson, H. (1994) *Children Speak: Children, trauma and social work*, Longman.

Cipolla, J., Benson McGown, D. and Yanulis, M. (1992) *Communicating through Play: Techniques for assessing and preparing children for adoption*, BAAF.

Cloke, C. and Davis, M. (1995) *Participation and Empowerment in Child Protection*, Pitman Publishing.

Colwell Report (1974) *Report of the Committee of Inquiry into the care and supervision provided in relation to Maria Colwell*, HMSO.

Department of Health (1991) *Patterns and Outcomes in Child Placements: Messages from current research and their implications*, HMSO.

Department of Health (1991) *Children Act Regulations and Guidance*, Vol 3, HMSO.

ESRC Study, *Children's Perspectives and Experiences of the Divorce Process*, Cardiff University (ongoing).

Fahlberg, V. (1994) *A Child's Journey through Placement*, BAAF.

Fratter, J. (1996) *Adoption with Contact: Implications for policy and practice*, BAAF.

Harper, J. 'Recapturing the past: alternative methods of life story work in adoption and fostering', in *Adoption & Fostering*, 20:3, pp.21–28.

Hill, M., Laybourn, A. and Borland, M. (1996) 'Engaging with primary-aged children about their emotions and well-being', in *Children & Society*, 10:2, pp.129–144.

Howe, D., Sawbridge, P. and Hinings, D. (1997) *Half a Million Women*, The Post-Adoption Centre.

Hughes, B. and Logan. J. (1993) *Birth Parents: The hidden dimension – The Evaluation of a Birth Parent Project*. Research Report commissioned by the Mental Health Foundation, University of Manchester, Department of Social Policy.

Ince. L. (1998) *Making it Alone: A study of the care experiences of young black people*, BAAF.

Lowe, N. (1997) 'The changing face of adoption: the gift/donation model versus the contract/services model', in *Child and Family Quarterly*, 9:4, pp.371–386.

Lowe, N., Murch, M., Borkowski, M., Weaver, A., Beckford, V., with Thomas, C (1999) *Supporting Adoption: Reframing the approach*, BAAF.

Marrow, V. and Richards, M. (1996) 'The ethics of social research with children: an overview', in *Children & Society*, Vol 10, pp.90–105.

Marsh, P. and Triseliotis, J. (1996), *Readiness to Practice: A training of social workers in Scotland and their first year of work*, Scottish Office, Central Research Unit.

Masson, J. and Oakley, M. (1999) *Out of Hearing*, Wiley.

Moore, M., Sixsmith, J. and Knowles, K. (1996), *Children's Reflections on Family Life*, Falmer Press.

Mullender, A. (ed) (1991) *Open Adoption: The philosophy and practice*, BAAF.

Murch, M., Lowe, N., Borkowski, M., Copner, R. and Griew, K. (1993) *Pathways to Adoption: Research project*, HMSO.

Neal, B., Wade, A. and Smart, C. (1998) *I just get on with it: Children's experiences of family life following parental separation or divorce*, Centre for Research of Family, Kinship and Childhood, University of Leeds.

NSPCC and Childline (1994) *Preparing Child Witnesses for Court*, NSPCC and Childline.

Quinton, D., Rushton, A., Dance, C. and Mayes, D. (1997) 'Contact between children placed away from home and their birth parents: research issues and evidence', in *Clinical Child Psychology and Psychiatry*, 2:3, pp.393–411.

Rushton, A., Quinton, D., Dance, C., and Mayes, D. (1998) 'Preparation for permanent placement: evaluating direct work with older children', in *Adoption & Fostering*, 21:4, pp.4–48.

Ryan, T. and Walker, R. (1993), *Life Story Work*, BAAF.

Ryburn, M. (1992) *Adoption in the 1990s – Identity and Openness*, Leamington Press.

Ryburn, M. (1998) 'In whose best interests? Post-adoption contact with the birth family', in *Child and Family Law Quarterly*, 10:1, pp.53–70.

Sachdev, P. (1991) 'The triangle of fears, fallacies and facts', in Hibbs (ed) *Adoption: International perspectives*, International Universities Press, Maddison CT, USA.

Schemmings, D. (1996) *Involving Children in Child Protection Conferences: Research findings from two child protection authorities*, Social Work Monographs, University of East Anglia.

Selwyn, J. (1996) 'Ascertaining children's wishes and feelings in relation to adoption', *Adoption & Fostering*. 20:3, pp.14–20.

Silverman, D. (1993) *Interpreting Qualitative Data: Methods for analysing talk, text and interaction*, Sage.

Social Services Inspectorate (1996) *For Children's Sake: An SSI inspection of local authority adoption services*, Department of Health.

Thoburn, J. (1990), *Success and Failure in Permanent Family Placement*, Avebury.

Thoburn, J., Murdoch A., and O'Brien, A. (1986) *Permanence in Child Care*, Basil Blackwell.

Triseliotis, J. (1973), *In Search of Origins*, Routledge and Kegan Paul.

Triseliotis, J., Shireman, J. and Hundleby, M. (1997), *Adoption: Theory, policy and practice*, Cassell.

Ward, L. (1997) *Seen and Heard*, York Publishing Services for the Joseph Rowntree Foundation.

Waterhouse, S. (1992) 'The role of the guardian *ad litem* in preparing the child for family proceedings', in Biggs, V., and Robson, J. (eds) *Developing your Court Skills*, BAAF.

Wolcott, H. (1990) *Writing up Qualitative Research*, Sage.

Useful Organisations

Below is a list of organisations connected with all aspects of the adoption process.

Adoption UK (formerly PPIAS)
Lower Boddington
Daventry
Northants NN11 6YB
Tel: 01327 260295
Supporting adoptive families before, during and after adoption.

ATRAP (Association of Transracially Adopted People)
c/o Post Adoption Centre
5 Torriano Mews
Torriano Avenue
London NW5 2RZ
Tel: 0181 672 8098
Information and support for people who have been transracially adopted.

BAAF Offices
Head Office and Be My Parent
Skyline House
200 Union Street
London SE1 0LX
Tel: 0171 593 2000

BAAFLink
MEA House
Ellison Place
Newcastle upon Tyne
NE1 8XS
Tel: 0191 232 3200

National Organisation for the Counselling of Adoptees and Parents (NORCAP)
112 Church Road
Wheatley
Oxfordshire OX33 1LU
Tel: 01865 875000
For adopted adults, and their birth and adoptive families.

Talkadoption
12-14 Chapel Street
Manchester M3 7NN
Tel: 0800 783 1234
A free, confidential helpline for young people (under 26) who have a link with adoption.

Post Adoption Centres
Organisations offering advice, counselling, information, training and self-help and support groups to adopted people, birth families and adoptive families.

Post Adoption Centre
5 Torriano Mews
Torriano Avenue
London NW5 2RZ
Tel: 0171 284 0555

After Adoption
12-14 Chapel Street
Salford
Manchester M3 7NN
Tel: 0161 839 4930

Merseyside Adoption Centre
316-317 Coopers Building
Church Street
Liverpool L1 3AA
Tel: 0151 709 9122

After Adoption – Yorkshire
31 Moor Road
Headingley
Leeds LS6 4BG
Tel: 0113 230 2100

West Midlands Post-Adoption Service
92 Newcombe Road
Handsworth
Birmingham B21 8DD
Tel: 0121 523 3343

After Adoption Wales
Unit 1
Cowbridge Court
58-62 Cowbridge Road West
Cardiff CF5 5BS
Tel: 01222 575711
and at
PO Box 64
Newtown SY16 4WF
Tel: 01686 622972

After Adoption Counselling Centre
Birthlink
Family Care
21 Castle Street
Edinburgh EH2 3DN
Tel: 0131 225 6441

Barnardo's Scottish Adoption Advice Service
16 Sandyford Place
Glasgow G3 7NB
Tel: 0141 339 0772

Useful Books

Below is a list of useful books published by BAAF except where indicated.

Books for children and young people

Children's book series
Sheila Byrne and Leigh Chambers

A new and unique series of books for use with children separated from their birth parents. The stories are simply told and attractively illustrated in full colour. Worksheets at the back of each workbook will help children to compare and contrast their own experiences with those of the characters in the story.

Joining Together: Jo's story, 1999.
Feeling Safe: Tina's story, 1998.
Living with a New Family: Nadia and Rashid's story, 1997.
Belonging Doesn't Mean Forgetting: Nathan's story, 1997.
Hoping for the Best: Jack's story, 1997.

Chester and Daisy Move On, 1995.
Angela Lidster

A delightful picture book about two bear cubs who go to live with a foster family and are then prepared to move to an adoptive family. For use with four to ten-year-olds.

Why Adoption?, 1995.
Kulwinder Sparks

Experiences to share for teenagers and their adoptive parents – adoption as seen from a young person's perspective.

Books for adults

Whatever happened to Adam?, 1998.
Hedi Argent

This remarkable book tells the stories of 20 young people with disabilities and the families who chose to care for them. All the "children" are now more than 20 years old and *Whatever happened to Adam?* follows their life journeys from joining their families, through childhood and adolescence and into preparation for adulthood.

Adopting a Child: A guide for people interested in adoption, 1998.
Prue Chennells and Chris Hammond. Revised by Jenifer Lord

Essential reading for anyone who is considering adopting a child, the book also includes a list of adoption agencies and details of other useful organisations.

Talking about Adoption to your Adopted Child, 1998.
Prue Chennells and Marjorie Morrison

This popular and comprehensive guide outlines the whys, whens and hows of telling the truth about an adopted child's origins.

Adopters on Adoption: Reflections on parenthood and children, 1996.
David Howe

This absorbing collection of personal stories of adoptive parents covers topics including assessment and preparation, feelings towards birth mothers and biology, infertility and parenting secure children.

The Adoption Experience: Families who give children a second chance
Ann Morris
Jessica Kingsley Publishers, 1999.
(Not available from BAAF.)

This book tells of adopters' experiences and follows through every stage of the adoption process.

After Adoption, Working with adoptive families, 1996.
Rena Phillips and Emma McWilliam (eds)

This unique anthology, illustrated with case studies, focuses on post-adoption support for adoptive families.

Advice Notes from BAAF

The Advice Note series contains essential information about the key areas of adoption and fostering.

Adoption – Some questions answered
Basic information about adoption – the process, procedures, the law and useful resources.

If You are Adopted
Answers to some of the questions adopted children ask, aimed at the children themselves. Includes information on tracing birth parents.

Intercountry Adoption – Information and guidance
Information on adopting a child from overseas, including procedures, legislation, and where to obtain advice and further information.

Stepchildren and Adoption (separate editions for England and Wales and Scotland)
Information on stepfamilies, the advantages or not of adoption, the alternatives and obtaining further advice.

Talking about Origins
An outline of adopted children's need to be told about adoption and the law on access to birth certificates.

For a free publications catalogue and details of prices for BAAF publications contact the Publications Department on 0171 593 2072.

Appendix A
Letter to parents

Adopted Children
Speaking

Mr & Mrs G. Armstrong
43 Weldon Road
Northampton
NH4 9KL

Cardiff Law School
University of Wales
PO Box 427
Cardiff CF1 1XD
01222 874644

26 March 1997

Dear Mr & Mrs Armstrong

Support Services for Families of Older Children Adopted Out of Care
Research Project

Some time ago you very kindly helped our research by talking to me about your experience of adoption support services. At that time I explained that we hoped later to study older children's views and experiences of adoption.

After careful preparation we are ready to begin this stage of the research. My colleagues and Caroline Thomas and Verna Beckford will be interviewing some of the children and I do hope you will feel able to help them.

As I mentioned when I saw you, we will be sending you a summary of our findings as soon as they are available. In the meantime, I hope all is well with you and your family.

With best wishes to you all.

Margaret Borkowski

Appendix B
Letter to parents

Adopted Children
Speaking

Cardiff Law School
University of Wales
PO Box 427
Cardiff CF1 1XD
01222 874644

10th June 1997

Mr & Mrs G. Armstrong
43 Weldon Road
Northampton
NH4 9KL

Dear Mr & Mrs Armstrong

'Adopted Children Speaking' Research Project

We are writing to ask if you will support Elizabeth's participation in 'Adopted Children Speaking.' The enclosed *Fact Sheet* outlines our approach. We hope that this tells you all you need to know and will make it easier for you to come to a decision. However, if, after reading it, you would like to discuss *any* aspect of the study, please contact us on 01222 874644. We will be glad to talk to you.

If you are happy for us to invite Elizabeth to take part, please give her the enclosed pack. We imagine that she might be puzzled by its arrival, so it may help her to know that you have already taken part in our project. The pack contains the leaflet and tape described in the *Fact Sheet* which should help Elizabeth to decide if she wants to participate. We have asked her to let us know her decision by returning a *blue* form in an enclosed pre-paid envelope.

We hope you will feel able to help us again. However, if you do *not* want Elizabeth to take part, please let us know by returning the *green* form enclosed. If we do not receive the blue or green forms within ten days, we hope it will be all right to follow up this letter with a phone call.

We look forward to hearing from you or Elizabeth.

With best wishes,

Yours sincerely,

Caroline Thomas and Verna Beckford

Adopted Children
Speaking

Fact Sheet for Adoptive Parents

If after reading this *fact sheet* you would like to discuss any aspect of the study, please contact us on 01222 874644. We will be glad to speak to you.

Project aims

- To study children's views and experiences of the support they received during their adoption
- To help the development of adoption support services for older children and their families

Interviews

Interviews will :

- be arranged over the phone
- usually take place at home, although other arrangements can be made if your child prefers
- normally be conducted on a one-to-one basis, but sibling groups can be interviewed together if appropriate
- last about an hour, but may be longer if your child has a great deal to say
- be tape-recorded

To explore adoption support we will ask questions about some of the stages of the adoption process. These stages include:

- preparation for adoption
- waiting to be adopted
- introduction to the family
- moving to a new home
- making the adoption order

We may also touch on contact with their birth and foster families and what it is like to be adopted now.

To help your child during the interview we have developed some materials that should make communication easier, even fun.

Findings

Full findings will be reported to the Department of Health by the end of 1997. Summaries of findings will be sent to all participating children and their families in 1998. Summaries will also be made available for social workers and other practitioners working in adoption.

The Children's Invitation Pack

These packs contain a leaflet and tape to let children know:

- who we are
- where we work
- why we want to speak to them
- what we want to talk to them about
- answers to possible questions
- that they can contact us if they would like to ask us any other questions
- that if they are not sure whether to take part, they can talk to someone else to help them make up their mind

Hopefully the packs will help your child make an informed decision about whether to take part.

Consent & Confidentiality

- once children have given their initial consent to be interviewed they can withdraw it at any time
- all information will be treated as strictly confidential

Adopted Children
Speaking

Cardiff Law School,
University of Wales,
PO Box 427,
Cardiff
CF1 1XD
01222 874644

Appendix D
Parents' response form

Adopted Children
Speaking

Cardiff Law School
University of Wales
PO Box 427
Cardiff CF1 1XD
01222 874644

If you do not wish your child to take part in the project, please send this form back to us in the envelope provided. Thank you.

Name

Comments

Appendix E
Children's explanatory leaflet

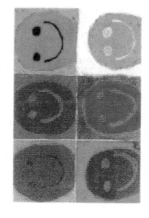

Adopted Children Speaking

An invitation to take part in a study of adopted children

Caroline Thomas   Verna Beckford

Whatever you decide to do, please send the blue form back to us. We hope to hear from you soon. Thank you.

Adoption Support Services Project
Cardiff Law School
University of Wales
PO Box 427
CARDIFF CF1 1XD
01222 874644

Smiles drawn by Hollie Grant, aged 11 years,
Colston's Primary School, Cotham, Bristol
Cardiff Law School 1996

We work together at Cardiff University and we're writing a book about children who've been adopted. To help us write the book we need to speak to lots of adopted children from all over the country.

We need your help. We'd like to talk to you about adoption. Who helped you the most? What made adoption easy or difficult for you? Would you like to change anything? We'd love to hear your answers to these and other questions.

We hope you'll be able to help us. By talking to you, we will be able to help other children who are going to be adopted in the future. This is your chance to help them too!

You may have some questions

How long do you want to talk to me?

For about an hour but if you've got a lot to say it could be more.

Will you tell anyone what I say?

Only the people we work with at the university.

Will you write down what I say?

Maybe, but we would like to tape what you say if that's OK.

Will anyone reading the book know me?

No one will know your name except us.

Will you both come to speak to me?

No, just one of us.

Can I change my mind?

Of course. You can change it at any time.

What if I'm not sure?

Take your time. Talk to someone else if that helps.

Can I talk to you first?

Yes. Just ring us on 01222 874644. If we're not there you can leave a message on the answer phone and we'll call you back.

Appendix F
Cassette tape sleeve

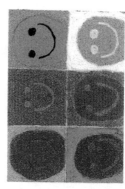

Adoption Support
Services Project
Cardiff Law School
University of Wales
PO Box 427
CARDIFF CF1 1XD

Adopted Children
Speaking

An invitation to take
part in a study of
adopted children

Adopted Children Speaking

Appendix G
Children's response form

Adopted Children
Speaking

Cardiff Law School
University of Wales
PO Box 427
Cardiff CF1 1XD
01222 874644

Whatever you decide to do, please send this form back to us in the envelope provided. Thank you.

Yes, I would like to help the **Adopted Children Speaking** project.

No, I don't want to help the **Adopted Children Speaking** project

Name

Appendix H
Children's consent form

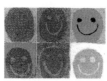

Adopted Children
Speaking

Cardiff Law School
University of Wales
PO Box 427
Cardiff CF1 1XD
01222 874644

CONSENT FORM

I agree to help out with the
Adopted Children Speaking project.

I do not have to answer all the questions.

I can stop the interview at any time.

Signed ....

Name   Caroline Thomas

Appendix I
Eco map

Appendix J
Prompt cards

This is to certify that

Holly Smith

took part in the
Adopted Children
Speaking
project

Adopted Children Speaking

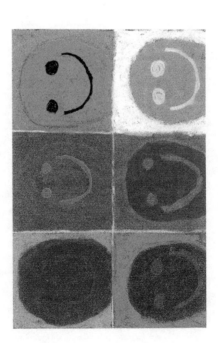

Could you adopt a child featured in
Be My Parent **or** *Focus on Fives?*

John Birdsall Photography/posed by models

There are thousands of children in the UK who are looked after by a local authority and who, for a variety of complicated reasons can never return to live with their birth families. All these children need new families. Like 12-year-old Zach who would benefit from one-to-one attention within a stable family environment. Or Chennelle, aged 3 and of white and African-Caribbean parentage and needs a new family with at least one black parent. Or Rachel who is 7 years old and hopes her new mum and dad will let her have a pet hamster.

You could help make a positive, lasting difference to a child like Zach, or Chennelle or Rachel through BMP's Family Finding Service.

Be My Parent is a bimonthly newspaper, featuring photographs and profiles of children who need new permanent families. It is available on subscription to families interested in adoption and long-term fostering.

Focus on Fives is a newsletter, available every two weeks to individuals and families who have already been approved to adopt or long-term foster children aged five years and under.

BAAFLink is a national database which links children needing permanent new families with families approved by agencies.

To find out more about adoption and fostering, *BAAF*Link, how to subscribe to *Be My Parent* and/or *Focus on Fives*, or to request a free information pack including a copy of the newspaper please contact:

Be My Parent
BAAF, Skyline House
200 Union Street
London SE1 0LX

Telephone **0171 593 2060**
Fax **0171 593 2073**
Email **bmp@baaf.org.uk**

B *ritish*

A *gencies*

for **A** *doption*

and **F** *ostering*

Registered charity number 275689
Limited company number 1379092